D0814944

Avoiding
THE SIN *of*
CERTITUDE

Avoiding

THE SIN *of*

CERTITUDE

A RABBI AND A THEOLOGIAN
in FEMININE INTERFAITH CONVERSATIONS
from DISPUTATION TO DIALOGUE

Rabbi Susan Talve & Carla Mae Streeter, OP

2020

Reviewed in SE 75,2023, 466-468.

Avoiding the Sin of Certitude is a series of dialogues between a progressive rabbi ordained in the Reform tradition and a Roman Catholic theologian. Both are women. The text is an attempt to shift from the usual mode of disputation to authentic dialogue, modeled on actual conversations that took place in private and in public forums over thirty years. The rabbi lives in St. Louis and is a wife, mother, grandmother and social activist. Her congregation is the only Jewish Synagogue located within the city limits of St. Louis. Carla Mae Streeter, OP, is a Dominican Sister of the Congregation of Catherine of Siena in Racine, Wisconsin. She is an emerita professor of systematic theology and spirituality at Aquinas Institute of Theology in St. Louis, where she has taught for thirty-five years.

Avoiding the Sin of Certitude: A Rabbi and a Theologian in Interfaith Conversations from Disputation to Dialogue

First Edition

Copyright © 2020 by Rabbi Susan Talve and Carla Mae Streeter, OP

Any part of this book may be freely copied and shared provided proper credit is given to the author(s), and reference is made to the publication.

Published by Rabbi Susan Talve and Carla Mae Streeter, OP
Central Reform Congregation, St. Louis
and Aquinas Institute of Theology, St. Louis
streeter@ai.edu

Printed in the United States of America
Cover design by Paraclete Press
Library of Congress Control number: 2020923063

ISBN 978-0-57880-788-1

9 780578 807881

DEDICATED
TO
Sister Rose Thering, OP
whose courage led us to seek the truth together

TO
Rabbi Robert Jacobs and Paul Reinert, SJ
*who made Jewish Christian Dialogue a Reality
in St. Louis*

Dr. Waheed Rana
Our friend

AND TO
Sister Antona Ebo, FSM
whose life was a witness of healing and hope for us all

TABLE OF CONTENTS

How does one disagree and not just "agree to disagree?" How do we begin with disputation, enter into discussion and engage in true dialogue? How do two strong women who are passionate about their very different religious identities find a common ground that their fire may burn for the common good? How do we avoid the sin of a too facile certitude that makes us deaf to the meanings and values of another? Can we remain faithful to our deepest convictions while keeping open to hear the other?

Our presentations and conversations over the past 28 years have pushed us to new insights and have changed us. They have deepened our own individual faith journeys and have created a bond of sisterhood. We trust that we will always be there as allies for each other. We are no longer "other."

In 2004, the St. Louis Jewish theater produced *The Disputation*, a play that reenacted the forced disputation of Barcelona between Nachmanides, Rabbi Moshe ben Nachman and Dominican Friar Pablo Christiani in July of 1263. Christiani, who was a Christian convert from Judaism, assured the King that he could prove the truth of Christianity from the

Talmud and other rabbinical writings. The Rabbi knew that if he won the debate his people would be tortured and if he lost they would be demoralized. It was a painful memory in history and one that left many feeling angry and ashamed. We were invited to respond to the play.

Sister Carla Mae Streeter, a Dominican theologian, and Susan Talve, a rabbi, could have continued the rancor of the unfinished disputation of so long ago. In fact, many in the audience would have liked to see that! But over the years we had committed to principles that would witness to another way of interacting, and guide us through the messiest of conversations.

- We would never participate in a polemic or a debate that set a tone of confrontation.
- We would strive to be collaborative, not competitive; nor would we apply pressure to try to change the other.
- We built in the expectation that our conversations would deepen us in our own faith by learning about and from the beliefs and practices of the other.
- We trusted that we would never use what we had learned to critique the other or her faith in conversation with others.
- We looked for opportunities to be allies while also respecting the boundaries of each other's differences.

flowing from the meanings and values beneath the garment. It is how we uniquely move in the world, how the world comes to know us wrapped in our garment. But in the body is a *soul*, the sacred space, with its psychic energy of dreams, of images, of imaginings, of deep emotion. This soul-energy powers our wonder, our inquiry, our judgments, our decisions. This energy prods us into soul-making, ever opening us into becoming more than we have been, never letting us settle for "enough." Then there is the *Soul-of-the-soul*. This is the Sacred Mystery itself, present in the inner sanctum of our own soul. This is where we are held in being by the One who "is."

Feminine Consciousness

When we went deep enough, we found there was a common source for our passion. As religious women serving in patriarchal paradigms, we shared the notion that the complete participation of the *feminine* is necessary for the healing and transformation of the planet. We both became convinced that the effort of women to be seen, to have their voices heard and their presence taken seriously, was still being side-tracked. The present feminine agenda is to achieve equality, to show the world that women can do what men do in all arenas including ministry. Helpful as it is, in this agenda the male is still the standard, and we came to understand that this is keeping all of us from the real agenda. The unaddressed agenda of the world, the synagogue, and the Church is the fact that we have not really probed the contribution of women to religion and culture in their own right *as women.*

FEMININE INTERFAITH CONVERSATIONS

From Disputation to Dialogue

It is our conviction that much dialogue results in getting tangled up in one another's garments. We trip over one another's beliefs, or rituals. We argue over the interpretation of our stories. It will be our intent to avoid this entanglement. We might say we will reverently lay the garment aside. It will be carefully folded and kept nearby to be taken up again. Now and then we will refer to it. However, we will, in a sense "divest." There is a body beneath the garment and a soul. And above all, there is the Soul-of-the-soul. We will try to find language to talk about these realities, even when we find ourselves stuttering on the way.

We will start with these *Starting Points:* deep listening, what we mean by "the garment," and the search for genuine feminine consciousness. We will then ask hard questions of one another about *Proselytizing and Evangelizing* and listen deeply to the answers. We will ask what *Sexuality, Intimacy, and Celibacy* are all about. We will probe for clarity about *Life's Beginnings and the Soul.* We will dare to enter the tense arena of *Stem Cell Research and Abortion.* We will explore together what we understand by *Sexual Orientation, Gender,* and *Race.* Finally, we will ask, in light of our own feminine consciousness, what real contribution women bring to the role of *Women in Ministry.* We invite you into these conversations, but even more.

Our conversations are a "dive into the depths." The reflections at the end of each chapter are an invitation for you to join us on this path. Perhaps together we can do our part to foster the task of healing the broken heart of the world.

CARLA MAE STREETER, OP
RABBI SUSAN TALVE

Avoiding

THE SIN *of*
CERTITUDE

CHAPTER ONE

LAYING THE FOUNDATIONS

STARTING POINTS

Deep Listening

Susan: Moses was an unlikely prophet. He could barely speak, but he was able to see the holy in the ordinary. We learn that he noticed that the bush was burning and not being consumed, and he stopped and turned aside. Because he was humble enough to notice and stop and turn, he came to know his destiny, and the path he would have to take for it to unfold. He was humble and reluctant, but the commentary tells us that he was chosen because when he was tending his sheep, if one strayed, he would follow and make sure it found its way back to the herd. God knew that Moses would not leave anyone behind. God knew that all who wanted to leave the narrow place of slavery would be included even if they had to be carried.

I used to think that the pivotal moment in the story was the turning and that turning just a little bit could hold the possibility of transformation, of something new coming into the world. It offers us the chance to change our path so that we do not make the same mistakes and hopefully find ourselves on a holier path. But then I noticed that the text says "*lo yishma-u,*" "we will not listen." The problem of the story, the cause of the suffering is because no one is listening. Moses doesn't listen to God, Pharaoh doesn't listen to God or Moses, the people don't listen to Moses. There are plenty of words but there is no listening. The teaching is that no matter how many words there are, how much talking there is, when no one is listening, the word is in exile. God is drawn into the story because God is listening; God hears the groaning of the people. But if we are not listening, all the words of dialogue, of forgiveness, and of hope are in exile and we remain in exile as well.

Carla Mae: This is what we must do in these conversations. We need to model the intense listening that takes us away from the disputation and the polemic. Rather than being motivated by a need to emphasize our own separate identities and defend our own turf, we come instead with the conviction that we need one another. We learn that there is something in this listening that gives us insights that will make our own traditions more whole. This listening helps us to experience our own faith in a deeper way than when we are isolated from each other. We must actively participate in this listening because the fullness of the word of God requires the listening ears of all of us listening together. I suspect that the unfolding drama of God's plan waits for this.

Susan: Listening to you describe your faith has helped me experience the faith of others. I remember attending the memorial service for the father of one of my daughter's friends. The Episcopal priest spoke about the sorrow of death, but he also spoke about the joy that the belief of resurrection and eternal life held for Christians. I would usually feel excluded by the Jesus language and imagery and tune out. But I pushed myself to listen and I recognized the deep faith in God he was sharing with the family. The garment of images was not mine, but I understood what he was saying and I felt comforted, especially when I could see that hearing his words helped the family. I was able to do this at that service because I have learned to feel safe with you and your "garment." I believe that if we were in a situation where my life or my faith were at risk you would be my ally. I would hope that you feel the same about me. I would lay down my life if yours was at risk. With our relationship and the relationships of so many others we hope that we can redeem the horror and the betrayal of the past.

Carla Mae: Listening to you I realize that our conversations open me up to a greater reality in my Christianity. We have a personal history with each other that makes this listening possible and allows a new spirit to emerge not in theory but in concrete situations. We have shared the treasures of our traditions with utter honesty and without the fear that you are going to call what I hold sacred inadequate or ridicule what I treasure. Nothing that I believe needs to take away from anything you are, and what you believe need not take away anything from who I am. Everything changes when listening is the mode of encounter. There is humility in listening. Arrogance has no patience with listening.

Identifying the "Garments"

Susan: The Jewish tradition warns about the dangers of taking scripture literally. We have different systems that guide us beyond the literal interpretation of the text to levels of understanding that inspire and transform our lives and our world. The Jewish mystical tradition suggests that the stories are a garment. The garment is necessary because without it we could never experience the deeper levels. Different religious traditions have different garments. Understanding the stories as garments allows us to embrace their imperfection and their brokenness. They reflect the material world filled with inherent flaws as well as wonder. Beneath the garment is the body. The body is made up of the laws and rituals that are also different in distinct cultures and faith traditions. At the level of the body we see how much we have in common as our rituals and laws attempt to mark meaningful life cycle passages in our lives. It is also the place we experience benign differences like different dietary laws and more challenging ones like polygamy, female circumcision, and capital punishment. But the garment, (the stories,) the body, (the laws and rituals) must not be mistaken for the soul. At the soul level we experience the essence of our beliefs and values. It is at the soul level we know that we have "come home" to a sacred space where we find the body and the garment that best fit us. When we are aware of the soul level, we understand that the body and the garment can be imperfect, and we are not meant to take them literally even though different traditions require more or less adherence to them. We recognize that they are necessary because of the distinctions that allow us to articulate the uniqueness of our experience. It is at this soul level that we truly dialogue. By sharing our stories and our traditions we become more aware of our own soul-songs and allow us to express these beliefs in ways that discuss and do not dispute. It is the sharing at this level that deepens each of us in our own faiths and helps us realize that we might not be able to do this work without the "other". At this level we may not agree but we can hear and understand. There is an even deeper level. That is the level of the Soul of the soul. At this level we are One in the Mystery. We are not "other." At this level we know that we are connected and that our differences are all part of a greater whole. Though we may never glimpse this level, believing that it exists will inform the song of the soul, the rituals and the laws and the garments that will one day reflect a global community that sees God in all humanity and all creation.

Carla Mae: I think you have given us a way to distinguish the inner core and the outer manifestations, the language that I've learned from my mentor, Bernard Lonergan, SJ. The body and the garment are visible. The soul and the Soul of the soul are deep realities that people today find difficult to express. This is intimacy language. But we are using the garment-body-soul and Soul-of-the-soul imagery to deal with real distinctions, and these distinctions, when not clear, have been a real source of tension among faith traditions.

Defining the "Feminine"

Susan: Through the years it has become clear that our conversations reflect the lens of feminine consciousness. We agree that the missing piece to human wholeness (shalom) is a balance of the masculine and feminine allowing for the spectrum of gender consciousness that is often repressed. As women in two distinct faith traditions it has never been enough for us to fit into the patriarchal constructs of stories and rules and rituals that we inherit. We recognize the imperfect balance determined by culture and feel called to add the voices of women's stories and experiences. We hope that our new garment will not include threads from the patriarchal traditions of the materialist, hierarchical cultures from which we have come. We are not satisfied with simplistic answers or fitting into male robes or roles. We recognize that the new garments will be different because women's roles will not be defined by the male authority. We also recognize that at the same time that women seem to have more freedom to participate in the structures of power throughout the world, we continue to suffer from discrimination throughout the world.

We agree that there is not one solution to the challenge of transforming society by including the feminine. As a Catholic theologian, you recognize the servant leadership of male priesthood that was set by Christ himself. You suggest that women seeking leadership ritually through ordination may be seeking too little. You warn that the ordination debate does too little to address the real issues of women. It has them seeking a male role. Settling for too little delays the weaving of a new garment. Women need to find their voices and places distinct from and yet in harmony with male authority and experience.

As an ordained rabbi, I claim my place in a patriarchal tradition that holds much wisdom, wonder and beauty for me. As a round peg in a square hole I find that I am part of the process that is pushing Judaism to be more inclusive. The ability to be responsive to the challenges of each generation and embrace progressive revelation has kept Judaism vibrant for generations. With the voices of women woven into the garment I feel the paradigm shifting in the religious realm toward a more inclusive experience for women and men. We have come to embrace the feminine value of *and/and* (both realities existing side by side) rather than the more confrontational *either/or* approach on the issue of ordination. One of my deepest beliefs is that we are giving birth to a new consciousness as we are letting go of a transcendent understanding of God that is separate from the world. In this view God dwells in a transcendent spiritual realm and shapes the physical world from beyond, allowing us to view both God and each other as "other."

I believe that as we begin to embrace a more immanent experience of God we will begin to experience the connectedness of all creation and be called in everything we do to reject the violence and injustice that is challenging our lives and the life of our planet. When we are taught to find the godliness inside and in the spaces between us, we will also begin to see the distinctions while understanding that the separations are illusion.

Carla Mae: I agree. And so, we have laid the foundations for our conversations. We will deeply listen, knowing that it is the person that makes the clothing beautiful, not the other way around. We will be watchful to avoid getting tangled in our own garments, and avoiding too, the temptation to clothe the other in our own garment. We will listen deeply to the body of rituals and laws that give our traditions a place in society, wearing the garment of our distinct experiences. Finally, we will try to be true to our own emerging feminine souls, the awareness and the wisdom this offers to both of us in our traditions and to the broader culture. Just maybe, we will catch a glimpse of the Soul-of-the-soul in our dialogue. This is the prescription for the lens we will use in our conversations. Our hope is that our respect and love for each other will inspire others to listen to those different from themselves. By these conversations we hope to begin the weaving of a new garment that deepens our faith and creates a shelter of peace for all creation.

Threads for the New Weaving

Susan:

We have the loom constructed, now we need to gather the threads to be woven. There will be themes to our conversations. We will be talking about proselytizing, intimacy, and the soul. We will discuss stem cells, sexual orientation and abortion. We will listen hard to each other on the place of women in ministry. But there is a foundational pattern guiding it all. This pattern is like a design that is presupposed by both of us. The pattern is taken for granted. But we need to begin by declaring it openly as best we can. Are there basic notions that will guide everything else we say? Will these basic notions harmonize? Will both of our perspectives blend to guide the weaving? Who is God for each of us? Where do we understand the world to be going? What wisdom does each of our traditions offer as a vision of the future?

The God and Human Partnership
THE DIVINITY OF JESUS AND TIKKUN OLAM/THE REPAIR OF THE WORLD

Carla Mae: For Christians, the Genesis narrative tells the story of the breaking of the most basic relationship, that of the human with God. The sin that leads to this loss mars the human. It is as if God can no longer see a reflection when looking into the human. It is as if God says, "You've destroyed my image in you by what you have done, so I will take *your* image to restore it." This is the new step. This is who Jesus is for the Christian. God brands God's self onto the human genome to get the point across of how serious God is about restoring this relationship. Jesus is the *way* it will happen, the *truth* of it, and the very *life* of God restored to humanity. It may be trite to see signs along the highway that "Jesus saves." But this is what folks who put them up are trying to say.

Just to be clear, it is God who does this by God's active Word. The humanity taken on is from Mary. God is Spirit. Human is human. This is a wedding, a marriage of humanity with divinity. The humanity of Jesus becomes the *instrument* of salvation. This gives us a clue. We humans do not do the saving. God is going to do it. Our humanness is the instrument for it to happen because we must be present in the world healing it. In a way God is saying, "You and I are going to do this together or it's not going to get done."

Susan: Jewish tradition offers many different interpretations of the meaning of the Garden of Eden. The one that resonates most with me says that it was a good thing for us to leave. In the Garden we had no purpose. Outside of the Garden our purpose becomes the repair of the world, what we call *tikkun olam*. The price we paid for a life of meaning was very high. But we are able to endure the suffering and mortality outside of the Garden because we are created in the image of God, *b'tzelem elohim*, and this encourages us to be our best selves even in the midst of an imperfect world. We are encouraged to act as co-creators with God. We work six days of the week to do the work of repair by observing the commandments and also by resting on the seventh day, the Sabbath, as God did. Our garments are different because we did not internalize the "sin" of the Garden as an act in need of salvation. Rather it taught us that we were given free will and that we would be encouraged again and again to choose the blessing over the curse, life over death, and good over evil. Religion is a fitness course for the soul, strengthening the inclinations to do good that we will respond in holy ways.

Carla Mae: In this sense I can affirm everything you say about this healing depending on what we humans do, and that it must take place here and now. I hear no contradiction in our stories. But I do hear different meaning as to how salvation takes place.

We Christians look at the world as coming from the hand of God as totally good. We learn that from our Judaic roots. That's the basis really for our understanding of the natural world as revelatory. We believe that the human is a free agent, and with free will has the capacity to thwart the plan of God. We believe the earth itself and the natural world are held hostage because the human thwarted the plan of God. The human being violated its own freedom by defying God in the Garden. This is our view of original sin. It's the original arrogance by which humans separated themselves from God and set themselves up as law unto themselves, as an idol. This narcissistic condition of the human who can freely choose, makes it necessary to ask, "Choose *what*?" How do we avoid a misuse of free choice coming from our woundedness?

The human is in a state of needing healing itself. The human is broken and wounded. But that does not, in the best of Christian tradition, say the human flesh or the human body or the human is bad. When Christian groups have equated the human with evil, or the body or what the body does with evil, that's usually a twisted form of Christianity. Salvation for the Christian is the *process* of our being healed, and redemption is what God did in Jesus to make it possible.

In other words, there's a deep conviction within Christianity also that the work is in this world. If you are clouded in your thinking, if you are paralyzed in your choosing, if you are confused emotionally, you can't fix yourself. God needs to free your condition sufficiently so that you can become the authentic human partner of God in your saving.

So the means or the way that God provides for that healing is to come personally to join the brokenness in the person of the Word. There is a total unity in God. Christians are not tritheists. We believe the very nature of God is revealed in three distinct but not separate relationships. There is a deep hidden mystery in the depth of God that is totally beyond human comprehension. This hiddenness, or this depth or heart of God, is called "Father," or in more abstract terms the "Source." Source is like a fountainhead, the very depths of the mystery of the divine. When this divine mystery expresses or reaches out to create the world: atoms, molecules, DNA, we distinguish the *thought* of it and the *power* to effect it. The thought or design is God's "Word." The power is called God's Spirit, the Holy Spirit of God. These three cannot be separated, for God is one, but they can be distinguished one from the other only *relationally,* not in any physical way.

An example might be fire. There is the flame, the light and the heat. We can distinguish, but we cannot separate these three. They are "in" one another in a relational union.

So the Word and the Spirit can never be separated, and they can't have any existence without coming from this hidden Source. We call this *perichoresis* in Greek - a dance within a dance, or *circumincession* in Latin. The creation of the universe is the expression of God acting through the Word by power of the Spirit.

Because Jesus in his humanness is the way back for us, this bond with humanity implies connection with every person. Not all Christians understand this. I believe that this gesture on the part of the Word, of taking on a Jewish humanness and fusing that to itself in an act of total self-emptying, merciful love, is the paradigm given to the human family for how God wants to unite with every culture, with every ethnicity, with every human being, with every group. I believe it is the paradigm for a restored divine/human intimacy. Jesus is to be broken open to show us what the destiny is for all of us. God unites with our struggle and our pain as we work toward the healing to come out of this condition of brokenness.

If we continue the hatefulness, we slow the divine plan down. We keep cultural progress from going forward because this is a communal thing, not just a Lone Ranger thing. Hatred and violence are toxic, they fuel the decay, the decline, the dehumanization, and the desacralization that continue to permeate human consciousness. This distortion comes through a twisted use of free choice. The misuse of human choice is not freedom but license. A responsible person needs to work through a lot of data today to make good choices. Even though that human freedom in its brokenness can be used to blaspheme, God still reveres it as a most sacred gift.

As religious people I think our role is to confront the *status quo* with very good questions that keep us growing as a human community. This role prevents me from being scandalized. I can see the depths of human brokenness reeking the most vehement, horrendous results and know there is another way.

An ancient bishop named Irenaeus said that human brokenness is natural. We must outgrow it the way we lose baby teeth. The famous Augustine disagreed. He taught that this wretched hateful condition has nothing to do with natural humanness but is, instead, sickness. The real human is *imago dei* and is good. The mainline tradition of Catholic Christianity is the Augustinian view that sin is not part of human nature. We don't get around our dastardly deeds by saying, "After all, I'm only human." To be fully human is to be someone who has never violated his or her own freedom. People can't even imagine that. They think our teaching about Jesus being sinless makes him inhuman. In other words, in their view, to be human you have to sin; sin is a necessary part of being human. Instead, as you sin you are capitulating to your sickness and calling it normal, calling it natural. Jesus is a paradigm of how we are supposed to be when we are whole.

Susan: One of my favorite texts is an 18th century ethical work called *The Path of the Just*, by Moshe Haim Luzzato. It's all about how you exercise the soul to be a better person. In the Talmud it says that the Torah leads to watchfulness. Watchfulness leads to zeal, zeal to cleanliness, cleanliness to separation, separation to purity, purity to saintliness, saintliness to humility, humility to fear of sin, fear of sin to holiness, holiness to the Holy Spirit, Holy Spirit to the revival of the dead. This is the path to becoming the best person we can become. Luzzato dedicates his whole book to taking this path, and the first part of the path is watchfulness. The first thing you have to master is this notion of watchfulness.

Carla Mae: Being attentive to your own self.

Susan: Yes. In many ways you and I have been practicing watchfulness with each other in our conversations. This practice requires that we remember that we are *b'tzelem Elohim,*in the image of God and to try to be more God-like in our actions. This means not giving excuses for our imperfections but knowing that our job here is to exercise the soul so that we can walk in God's ways. Luzzato says, "Let there be implanted in a person's heart a love for God which will arouse your soul to do what is pleasing to God." The next step is wholeheartedness, a dedication to divine service where your interests are not divided, and your observance is merely mechanical. In this step your whole heart must be devoted to divine service. The observation of the *mitzvot* becomes your whole self observing the commandments in a way that draws godliness into the world so that you really become a co-creator with God.

Carla Mae: You become a door and a gate for holiness.

Susan: We say it is becoming a vessel to channel holiness into the world.

Carla Mae: It's very interesting to hear Jesus, coming out of his Jewishness, saying similar things. What you have described puts them in context. He says, "I am the gate." "I am the door." "I am the way." This is no sweet plastic Jesus. This is a divine human bridge. We are challenged to get something done. He says in the garden to his disciples, "Watch and pray with me." And they all fall asleep, of course. It's interesting to me as a Christian that he does not exclude them because they fail. I think he's a bridge to help us understand that holiness comes from God *through the Jews* because he chose to identify with them.

Susan: Practically speaking, a Jew must ask of the Christian, "Can I be a vessel even if I am on a different path?" Does one have to have the understanding that this happened through Jesus? Can there be other ways for us to receive and give the healing we need? It makes me nervous that your garment, your story, needs the "Jews" as a vessel.

Carla Mae: I think this is Soul-of-the-soul territory. We need to check our experience. Healing is going on. It is going on for the Buddhists, for example. It is going on for the Jewish community. It is going on even as the Jews face what has happened to them since the Holocaust. It is happening, right now, with the Islamic community, in the face of all the fundamentalism, all the terrorism. It is going on through humanness. Either there is some truth in this pattern of how God works, or there isn't. Whether we talk about it in terms of Jesus or not is not going to stop it from going on. We need to seek out the truth. We will all know one day.

Susan: In the Jewish community we are still waiting for a messianic time when we will live in peace. Some believe it will be a messiah, some a messianic age, but we all agree that the proof will be that we will be living in peace.

Carla Mae: I go back to *The Disputation,* where Nachmanides says, "You say this has happened. You say the messiah has come. Look at the world. Does it look like it's saved or redeemed?" He had a point. If you say your Jesus did this, then why isn't it showing, why isn't it present in the world? As a Christian I answer that we are still catching on. The sin of the Church, the sins of Christians prevent it from shining through. Why do I say this? Because it must come by way of the human. If there is no partnership, there will be no change.

Susan: I have no trouble with messianism as long as I can put my own garment on it. We call it *tikkun olam.* Our participation in this mystery through the mitzvot is *tikkun* *olam*, repairing the world by drawing God's attributes into the everyday business of living. This is how we bring about that transformation. We just have a different story, a different garment. I believe it is the same essence. I believe it is the same teaching. It is our responsibility to repair the world and we are always in search of the most effective strategies to bring this about and critique those that create barriers.

Carla Mae: The mystery of the holy that is working in the world has been working since before the Christian and Jewish traditions. God has been mightily patient with the likes of us. We think we've got it all figured out. We need a basic humility to come to know one another. Once you visit my house maybe I can say things in a way that you might be able to hear, and you can say things to me that I'm not going to judge immediately as false or wrong. Basic humility respects the mystery that holds us both. It makes us ready to be open to serve.

Susan: I think this notion of the incarnation, the way that you have described the god/human partnership, is really very close to what I would say is the purpose of life. When I first came to St. Louis, every time I would hear someone praying in Jesus' name I would cringe. Remembering what was done in Jesus' name historically especially to the Jews, created a great barrier. But your explanation that the purpose of the Jesus narrative is to bring about the transformation of a broken world to a world of wholeness and peace feels familiar. That is messianism for me. That's the understanding that builds a bridge to a better world. When we realize that we are both working for the repair of the world, then we can see beyond the differences, find this as a common truth, and make room for each other.

Messianism for me means being inclusive. That's why it was so important for Central Reform Congregation to be in the city and for us to be welcoming to those who had been marginalized. This also led us to honor the integration of the personal and the political. One of the catch phrases for us as Jews is "Next year in Jerusalem." You have heard it at our seder table. But what does it really mean? Is it a metaphor for everyone to find a spiritual home, or inner peace, or the world to come, or to find their way to heaven? Or is it a political hope that all people will one day live in peace with each other and the environment? I would suggest that for the Jewish people it is political. The messiah in the rabbinic period was not a divine figure. It was a political figure, a descendant of David who would become a great leader and lead us to a time of peace.

The philosopher Maimonides said, "We long for the days of the messiah not in order to rule over the world and not to bring others under our control but to have time to study Torah with no one to bother us." The rabbis throughout the ages came up with their visions of peace and most of them are about finding a way to have what they need so that they have the leisure to study Torah.

Carla Mae: Which would say that they have space for contemplation, or they have space for prayer and reflection and that is taken from you when you are besieged or when you are oppressed.

Susan: Yes, exactly. Maimonides says, "In that age there will be neither famine nor war nor envy nor strife for there will be an abundance of worldly goods. The whole world will be occupied with the knowledge of God." If there is no change in the worldly order of things how will we know? And his answer is "by historical success." This is always the debate between Jews and Christians. If Jesus came as the messiah, why are things such a mess? This is really where that comes from. We will know that the messiah has come because there will be peace outside and in. It will not just be some that are able to devote their lives to this knowledge of God, to contemplation and prayer, but everyone will. Also, in Maimonides' view, we will no longer need catastrophe to occur first. There won't have to be suffering to gain knowledge. But a time will come when we will be able to just sit down and study Torah together. In our tradition we say that the message of the prophets is all about the messianic age and how to bring it about. For them it is quite simple. There will be a re-establishment of the house of David. All nations will turn away from idolatry and toward God and there will be a resurrection of the righteous, and then, finally, there will be everlasting peace. But before all this can happen, according to the prophets, there will be a great catastrophe, and only at the moment of deepest despair, they said, will there be a chance for redemption. But of course, that was their experience. The prophets experienced the destruction of the Northern Kingdom and the exile of the Southern Kingdom. They hoped that destruction and suffering would eventually lead to redemption. I hope that we have evolved beyond the need for a catastrophe to lead to redemption because the weapons that we have are more serious than they ever would have imagined.

Carla Mae: They will destroy the planet if they are really let loose. They will destroy us, not just our enemy.

Susan: The Talmud gives us a different image and tells us that we will find the messiah at the gates of the city tending the wounds of the lepers.

That's where we need to look. We can't look only in those places of academia or contemplation because until everybody has the leisure to study the knowledge of God it's not what we're talking about. If you are going to look for the messiah today when the world is still broken, you have to look for the messiah with Mother Theresa. You must look for the messiah in the work of Heschel who prayed with his feet when he marched with Dr. King. But I do hope that there are other ways than suffering to learn and be motivated to do the work of repair.

Carla Mae: Suffering does determine faith or disbelief for a lot of people. It's the theodicy question, the question of evil and suffering. If suffering has been part of the human condition, we need to see a purpose for this suffering and see how this fits into the whole cosmic picture. If we look at the entire cosmos there seems to be a rhythm that is built in. A star collapses and out of the star's collapse comes an entire universe. A seed dies in the ground and a whole new plant comes from the seed that had to die and break apart. It's a pattern. The mother carries a child and then has to go through this terrible pain of separation from this creature that has become so dear. It needs to have a life of its own. And then eventually the mother dies. This is the pattern we see repeated and we wonder where the divine is in all of this. What does the divine have in mind? Is it from the outpouring of the divine itself in some type of sacrifice that love gets its name, its identity? With God, there is no love until there is the giving until nothing is left. It's a great mystery. For me it's tied up with suffering. I don't think about the question of evil anymore as abstract. I distinguish between this natural rhythm of birthing and dying from malicious evil that we spawn from our own choices. In our relationship with God there is something so great that no amount of this evil is going to thwart it, no amount of evil is going to have the last say.

Susan: I believe that evil exists only where we make room for it. In the mystical tradition we imagine that there is an overflowing of God's *attributes* that flow into the world, and these emanations of God are all defined as good. Evil attributes only exist in the human heart. Greed, pride, arrogance, and the kinds of things that cause such suffering communally don't exist outside of us. They only exist inside of us, which is hopeful because then if they only exist inside of us then we can do something about them.

Our challenge is to be channels for these attributes of godliness that we know exist. One of the ways we do that is through prayer, study, awareness and acts of loving kindness as our traditions define them. When the Baal Shem Tov was asked, when will the messiah come, his answer was, "When your wellsprings are overflowing." I think what the Baal Shem Tov was trying to tell us is that inner and outer peace will come when everyone is satisfied. We both know people who tell us that they feel empty inside. The truth is that no one is truly empty. Within each of us is the Soul-of-the-soul or God. When we come to know this, we become a channel for these attributes of godliness. When our wellsprings are overflowing, whether we have a lot or a little, we have what we need to be co-creators with God in the repair of the world and whatever personal suffering comes our way we can still respond in holy ways and not be destroyed by it.

Carla Mae: What I hear you saying is that in Reform Judaism the messiah is not necessarily understood as one person, but the entire community acting together.

Susan: That's exactly right. The teachings of Torah and the commandments guide us to do our part to bring the messianic age.

Carl Mae: The mystics in the Christian tradition would say that this life is a school to learn loving. It is in the Christian life of caring for others that compassionate love goes out. That's why Mother Teresa is such an epitome of what Christians ought to be doing. She said you do not have to come to India. You've got lonely and poor in your own neighborhoods. What she was doing is just telling the Christians to take seriously what they should know in the first place. What they see in her is exactly what Jesus was trying to say. You must become me in your own flesh, in your own life. When that happens, then I shall be all in all, and you and I together shall be one. The Jesuit, Teilhard de Chardin, says there's going to be an omega point reached. Nature shows us that there's always a mounting of complexity. He maintains that evolution doesn't stop at the physical level; it continues at the spiritual level. What we are moving toward is a cosmic Christ which is a humanity that is permeated by the Spirit of God and is like a lighted lamp. In the Christian scriptures, in the book of Revelation, this reality is called the New Jerusalem. It comes down as a bride from heaven and it's foundation are the prophets and the gates around the city are the twelve apostles. There is no need for a sun and moon because the living stones and the people radiate the light from the Lamb. A Lamb is in the middle of the city and the Lamb is slain. This is of course the Christ who has shown the epitome of self-giving sacrificial love in his death on the cross. This becomes the lamp, the new city, the new earth. The words are "I make all things new. The former heavens and earth pass away and I make all things new." This is in the book of Revelation, the last book of the Christian scripture. It's a very profound mystical piece. When it has been interpreted literally it has been misused. These are great mysteries. Do we have to have such stunted imaginations? Why do we have to be so confined to what we think is possible or impossible? The book of Revelation says there will be no tears, there will no suffering, there will be no war against one another. So, in our partnership with God and our imaginings of messianism, I hear many common threads. They are the threads of inclusivity, of hope, of direct human action, and of divine activity. Jesus has a marvelous line at the last supper. He says, "In my father's house there are many mansions." So, Susan, please come visit my house, as I have come to visit at your house. Where are those mansions but in God?

Susan: We have a teaching that says that the heart has many chambers. This teaches us that as we imagine and weave different garments, all is in God. The way Moses knew God was *panim el panim,* face to face. This teaches us that for us to know God we must look into the face of the other and find God in the communion, the relationship between us.

Carla Mae: We can agree that all is in God. And yet, your garment is distinctly yours and mine is mine. The goal we seek is common to us both. We seek a healed world.

Susan: I believe it is not an accident that two women open to deepening our own faith journeys by listening to each other are having this conversation at this point in time. I hope that there is a process unfolding where the sharing of faith as we see it through our own lenses, modeling listening that is non-threatening, will be a part of the evolution needed for a more just, a more inclusive and a more loving world.

Carla Mae: Amen.

TWO

SALVATION

PROSELYTIZING VS. EVANGELIZING

Susan: I remember mentioning to you that I was going to Mexico. You told me how you loved Bartolome de las Casas and his book, *Love Alone*. As good as his book sounded, all I could think of was why he had to impose Christianity on the indigenous people. Intellectually I understood that when you have something that you value you want to share it. That is when we had our conversation about how one can share information without pressing for, or forcing, conversion.

Carla Mae: I believe that what is precious in one's own tradition can only be shared by invitation. Proselytizing is pressing one to convert while true evangelization is an invitation to come see what I treasure without coercion, without manipulation.

But we Christians have not always practiced this. History has many examples of coercion.

There has been a tremendous change in what we call missiology, the mission of the Christian community. This new understanding of evangelization is actually written in a document called *Evangelii Nunciandi, The* Evangelization of Peoples, written by Paul VI, the leader of the Catholic community who succeeded John XXIII. As Roman Catholics we do not use the word "proselytizing". In fact, that word is pejorative to an educated Catholic because the word automatically brings in an element of coercion or manipulation. It is as if I were saying you have got to accept what I'm saying or you are worthless, or worse that you are damned or lost. It is true that some Catholics and other Christians will speak this way because they interpret scripture or Church documents with this lens. What is important here is to seek the *official* Church's opinion. This can be done by checking actual Church documents and their interpretation by the leadership and scholars of the Church.

The important realization is that people at times cannot accept what you are saying. And this doesn't mean they are against the truth. It means that at some level they cannot connect with what we are telling them we think the truth is. We have been learning that we cannot use a dogmatic hammer to change people. Real change comes only by accepting from within. It reminds me of the teaching about Moses turning at the burning bush. He turned and his life changed. God called to Moses through the bush and yet, Moses had to do the turning. The true position of the Church is to allow people to turn on their own, even though this is not the way it has always been practiced in the past. Sharing the "Good News" is vital to the mission of Christianity, but this mission is not approached the same by all of us. Some Catholics are still pretty manipulative, even though the Church has made its position pretty clear in print.

Susan: One response of the Jewish community to this mission is to ask if there is only *one way*. Does one have to accept this "Good News" to be right? You started out by saying that it is your conviction that for the wholeness of the truth it's necessary to have all of our voices to heal the heart of the world. This is a very Jewish view. There have been very few times in Jewish history when we have imposed our way upon others. Jewish tradition supports the notion that one doesn't have to be Jewish to be righteous or have a place in the world to come. We are not here to make the whole world Jewish. But I still hear that there is only *one way* of being "saved" in the Catholic Church. Does one need to be baptized to be saved? Whether you want to baptize me out of love or by coercion, help me understand how can we really all be necessary and have a common ground if you believe that?

Carla Mae: The key is *how* I believe that. There are Christians who will believe it just that way—in or out. You say the words, you pour the water, you're in, that's it. But that is the level of the *body* (the ritual and the rules). But what about desire, what about longing for God? What about Abraham and Moses and all those Holy Ones who were not baptized ritually, yet scripture says about Abraham that his faith justified him? Let me come at this from a different direction with a story. Clarissa Pinkola Estes, the woman who wrote *Women Who Run with Wolves,* was expecting a child out of wedlock and was sent to a convent as she was waiting to give birth. The young women were carefully instructed on the rules. The procedure was to be that after labor and the birth, the mother would then give the child up for adoption without seeing the baby. When her time came, Clarissa grabbed the nurse's arm with the words, "I want to see my baby!" As the nurse turned, Clarissa dipped her finger in the tears running down her own cheeks, made the sign of the cross on the baby girl's forehead and said the words that she knew, "I baptize thee..." Though the child would be taken from her, connecting with her in that way assured her that they would be reunited in the world to come.

Within the Catholic Christian tradition there is a very profound understanding of belonging, of being *part* of something. This is much more profound than asking, "Are you saved?" and getting a quick answer. This is our ritual of belonging and of being part of the group. When you are totally cut off from the group there is no hope, you are "lost." Now each of us knows that in our families there are members who are connected in various ways. Some are there for everything, in on everything, and central. Others are rather "fringy." They show up — sometimes. They are there or not there because they either want to be or not.

What is the desire of faith-filled people who are not Christians? Am I going to place myself as judge of their desire? I understand that as quite arrogant. So, are you saved, Susan? Do you desire God with all your heart? Are you a sincere believer? I think you have the answer to your own question, even though you are not at my side in my conviction that Jesus is the final revelation of God's Word, imprinted on human DNA, a living text. Nor have you experienced ritual water baptism. Perhaps you have been baptized with your own tears of longing.

Susan: This changes the whole conversation. Rather than asking are we both saved, we are now asking if there is room for both of us to belong. This is weaving a new garment that we share. Being cut off from the community is the most serious consequence in my tradition as well. In fact *galut*, exile, is the opposite of *geulah*, redemption. *Ga'al Yisrael*, the Redeemer of Israel, is a name for God. What does *geulah*-redemption- mean for us? Does it mean inner peace, or does it mean that we believe that there will be a messianic age when all creation will live in peace? Is redemption a state of being, a moment in time or the end of days? I can find Jewish texts to support all these ideas. I find it useful to consider the opposite of redemption. For me, the opposite of *geulah*, redemption, is *galut*, exile. The root of *geulah*, to redeem can also mean to act as a kinsman, suggesting that it is about acting as a community and belonging to each other. The root of *galut*, exile, can also mean to be revealed, made naked or become vulnerable. Anyone that is outside the circle is in exile and vulnerable. When we are inside the circle we are redeemed and, as family, we do what we need to do for the common good. Redemption is a communal notion that takes place in this world and you don't have to be Jewish to be in the circle. When Clarissa baptized her baby with her tears she was making sure that her baby would be inside the circle.

Carla Mae: So, redemption from the Jewish perspective is something that humans are deeply involved in. In other words, redemption does not just come from a transcendent distant God on high.

Susan: The experience of redemption is intimate and personal. The whole story of Exodus is about the ending of personal and communal exile. We are redeemed when we personally connect to the story and make room for all in the circle. All the laws of Torah are about how we can live together peacefully, in community, once we are brought in from exile.

Carla Mae: Being included can come, according to Catholic teaching, by raw desire, by ritual water baptism which brings one in institutionally, or by blood shed for one's beliefs. Baptism can be looked upon as a kind of ritual magic or it can be looked at in a much deeper way as an inclusion among the folks who live by faith. So maybe we need to ask, who is really "in" that we have thought was "out?" And maybe the tent of belief is wider than we thought, and some of the people we once thought were "out" will all be there. Maybe our desire has linked us with God and with a deeper family of believers than we once understood. This is not to dismiss ritual baptism into a specific Christian community as unimportant at all. It just asks the question of deeper meaning. And included in that is the question of how the millions of people who have never been ritually baptized, most likely including Jesus' own mother, be excluded from the heart of God? How can so many be excluded from salvation? This is an example of how we get tangled in our *garments.*

Susan: What do you mean by salvation?

Carla Mae: That is the question! God makes the opening, this is redemption. When we chose to walk through, this is salvation. For us then, salvation is a process, and it begins here in this life by making personal choices. It ends with a final transformation of our humanness by resurrection in the life to come. This change, we believe, takes place immediately upon death outside of time, but will be manifest to everyone in time at the event we call the *final judgment.* This event takes place at the end of time as we know it.

So, my question to you, Susan, is could you too be in process of being "saved?" As I know you, you are already giving evidence of godliness, of being transformed by love. Could this be happening to you even though you would not speak of it in the way I do? Even more challenging, is this completion in you powered by Jesus' resurrection or not? I would say yes. But

I can't insist you see it that way. I guess one day we will both find out where the full truth lies, yes?

This is why a Catholic Christian will not be boxed in by a simple "yes" to the question, "Are you saved?" The Catholic Christian who understands salvation as a process would probably say something like, "I am being saved." This reply would be more truthful, for the process is not completed until one passes over to the next life.

What keeps the process going is grace. Grace, for the Catholic, is the gift of God's own self permeating and influencing my day to day life. God's presence accommodates to each of us. My favorite image is oil creeping up a Kleenex. It's wonderful to watch. When you dip the end of the Kleenex in the oil it slowly climbs. The Kleenex is still Kleenex, but it will never be the same, because it's getting oiled. Something like that happens as the presence of God permeates a person's conscious life. They remain the same, but not really. They are graced. Their humanness is still there, but it is being transformed into something loving, selfless, forgiving, and courageous, something more than it could be on its own without God. Grace is the restoration of the relationship with God that we lost by wanting to be in control, by wanting to be on an equal par with God too soon. I agree that we were meant to leave the Garden to be in relationship with God, but I would say that we left too soon. We were still too self-centered.

Arrogance got in the way of us maturing into the friendship and intimacy with God that we call grace.

Our scriptures point to a time when there will be a new heaven and a new earth. The book of Revelation, the final book of the Christian scriptures describes it. It is all about transformation. I often wonder whether this is really pointing to the culmination of evolution. What are we evolving *toward*? The Jesuit, Teilhard de Chardin, a paleontologist, wrote that all the cosmos was ascending toward an omega point. He understood this as all atomic structure moving toward an upward development. He finds evidence for this in the physical world. Lower life forms move toward more complex forms. He believes that is happening on the psychic and spiritual as well as physical levels.

Susan: I too believe that we are reaching toward a more intimate and mature relationship with God that will come with our human transformation. Though Judaism is firmly rooted in law and tradition, there is always a way to reach infinitely outward and infinitely inward through the progressive revelation of interpretation and commentary of the text. We do not just put what we call a fence around the Torah by adding laws that keep the *mitzvot*, the commandments, protected. We also trust in the process of *midrash*, the delightful, imaginative responses to questions that come up in the text. There is a recognition of progress through thought and through serious study that produces a *chidush*, something new. Maimonides, the medieval philosopher says that when the prophet Isaiah proclaims that "the wolf shall dwell with the lamb and the panther shall lie down with the kid," it doesn't mean that the order of the world will change or that there needs to be a radical change through a great upheaval or a catastrophe in the world. Rather, Maimonides, the philosopher-rabbi, who was also a physician, says "this means that Israel will dwell securely even among those who have done her harm." In the metaphor, those who have done her harm are the wolf and the panther. In the messianic age we will understand what the metaphors of the Bible mean. Then the order of the world will not have to change; *we* will change. Like Chardin, this suggests that human beings have to transform, or evolve, to live more in harmony with the natural world and to be in the intimate relationship with God.

Carla Mae: I'd like to suggest three metaphors that for me demonstrate three views of how we are "saved." Every religion I know favors one view or another.

The first metaphor is that of the tortoise. In the moonlit night the tortoise mother comes ashore, and with her back flippers digs a deep hole in the sand. Into the hole she lays her leathery eggs. She covers them with sand, returns to the sea, and is seen no more. The eggs hatch, the baby turtles make for the ocean, and if the gulls don't get them, the little turtles continue the cycle. The eastern religions might find this metaphor captures their understanding of "saving." It is dependent on the creature itself, there is no outside savior, and the focus is on self-realization.

Next, we can find insight in the metaphor of the tiger. Ever watchful, the mother tiger keeps a keen eye out while the cub plays happily on the jungle floor. But should the mother sense the thundering approach of a rhino on a rampage, in a flash the cub is picked up by the scuff of the neck and carried off to safety. As for the cub, it curls up and allows itself to be saved. There are traditions that believe safety for the human is all God's doing. Human response is merely passive. The work is really all God's.

Finally, there is mother and baby monkey. Mom is swinging from vine to vine above junior who is eating a banana on the jungle floor. Along comes the tiger. Down swings mom, away goes the banana, and junior grabs the hair on her chest and is carried up into the treetops. Notice the action. Nothing would happen if mom didn't take the initiative. But the action would not be completed if junior didn't respond, but just continued to chomp away on the banana. There is the primary action of God saving, but the free human response is a part of the full act of saving. This latter metaphor captures the Catholic view, which takes human freedom very seriously as part of the saving.

Susan: When considering salvation, I lean in the direction of the monkey as well. I find myself thinking of the story of Eve, in Hebrew, Chava, a name that suggests mother of all life. When I read the story of the creation narrative, I am grateful to Eve for getting us out of the Garden. Yes, the price is great, (mortality, hard work and suffering even in childbirth,) but the reward is a life of meaning. Inside the Garden, we had no meaningful work. But outside we are co-creators with God. We are necessary for the work of *tikkun olam*, the repair of an imperfect creation. I do love the idea that you have suggested that we were meant to leave the garden, but we left a little too early, before we were ready to have a mature relationship with God. This understanding of the story is a great example of how our dialogue at the level of soul is helping us to weave a new garment.

It is in this context that I understand salvation. I personally believe that the soul continues to exist after the death of the body but in Judaism there are many different beliefs about this. Both redemption and salvation are understood in the context of how we live this life. According to the Talmud a question we would be asked in heaven is how we behaved in the marketplace. Were we honest in business? We recognize that within us there is a struggle between the inclination to do good and the inclination to take shortcuts, to miss the mark and not be our best selves. The *mitzvot*, the commandments, serve as a fitness course for the soul, strengthening our inclination to do good so that when we are confronted with the opportunity to respond in holy ways to the brokenness and the suffering around us, we will not stand idly by. I too, would choose the paradigm of the monkey and its mother, for humankind and God, the will of both is necessary for the salvation of the individual and the redemption of the community that leads to the transformation of the culture of non-violence that we desire.

Another teaching that reveals the Jewish notion of salvation comes from Exodus 6:6 and gives us the ritual of the four cups of wine in the Passover Haggadah. God tells Moses, I will bring you out, I will deliver you, I will redeem you and I will take you to Me. Each promise becomes a cup of wine and a step that takes us out of the narrow place of slavery and puts us on the journey toward liberation and freedom and the intimate mature relationship with God we are reaching toward. The four promises also give us a guide to personal and communal salvation. The first step is to become unstuck and leave the narrow place behind.

The second, the delivering, is not just to take the people out of slavery but to take the slavery out of the people. The third is redemption which here means to end the exile and to become a valued part of the community. The fourth cup represents our being taken into God. We come to know the power of faith and feel God's love despite the brokenness and imperfection around us. And, as always, there is one more promise. The fifth promise is, I will bring you into the land. The promised land is our metaphor, our garment, for the kind of peace that we can have knowing that we are living our lives intentionally and with meaning. Doing the work of *tikkun olam*, the work of repairing the world, saves us because it gives us peace. I believe that it is no accident that the path to this peace is attached to the blessing we say over the cups of wine, our symbol of the joy that comes from living a life of meaning. If this is what you mean by asking me if I am in the process of being saved, of making the choices that keep me on the journey, I would answer that our garments may be different, I may not speak of Jesus or the salvation in his resurrection, but I have no doubt we are on this path together.

Carla Mae: It is also part of our garment that redemption is from the Jews. We believe that the Word came to humanity through a Jewish particularity. Jesus came through a people that has suffered public persecution and heinous acts. Why were they chosen? I don't know. But Christians must ask themselves, "Why was it this people that the Word chose?" if we are true to our own revelation.

Susan: Yes, but practically, from the Jewish point of view, this being chosen, has only caused us more suffering. When we talk about slavery in Egypt we don't blame the Egyptians, in fact we remember their suffering at Passover. We blame Pharaoh, the great divider, not the Egyptian people. But the New Testament accounts blame the Jewish people and the Jewish leaders for the death of Jesus.

Carla Mae: Right, we did. But not anymore, and that's official.

Susan: Okay, I stand corrected. But that part of the Christian garment is still a challenge.

Carla Mae: Anti-Semitism does not die by a declaration because it is so ingrained.

Susan: This is why many people object to using the term *Judeo-Christian tradition*. I don't want to be part of the Christian story. Let Christians have their story and their faith and their garment and bring peace to the world in their way. It just does not feel fair that we have to be part of a story that puts us in a vulnerable position. It feels manipulative and abusive.

Carla Mae: If I can speak from my limited Christian perspective, I really think you have reason to feel that way, because at that time we were still stuck in our anti-Semitism very strongly, and we did use the Jewish community as a scapegoat reflecting an arrogant perspective. I would hope that in mainline Christianity, among those who know better, this is no longer acceptable.

Susan: But look at the millions of people who are using Mel Gibson's *Passion of the Christ* to teach the story. When I walked out of that film, I heard people saying "Now I know the real story." He used that narrative to highlight every Jewish stereotype from the Middle Ages. I know there are other things in the story to consider, but it's really hard to see them as a Jew. All I saw were little Jewish kids turning into devils, Jewish women looking like nuns in their habits, and Jewish men looking like horrible medieval Shylock rabbi-types with their prayer shawls over their heads. The Jews are the bad guys. It's pretty hard to take.

Carla Mae: The role of religious leadership in the Christian community, and I consider myself one of those leaders, is to teach its people the official position on this. Also, if an artistic depiction like this comes out like the Da Vinci Code which critiques the Church, it is the role of people who are educated in their religious communities to speak out as well.

Susan: This brings up the question of how each of our traditions views suffering. I would agree that suffering comes from the imperfection of creation. It is the price we pay for living in a material world but as co-creators with God, our work is to relieve suffering as much as we can. The point of the story of Job from a Jewish perspective is to make sure that we do not fall into the trap of believing that suffering is a punishment from God. Jobs' friends are convinced that he must have done something to deserve all his suffering. We know that he has done nothing. This is not to say that our actions do not bring about consequences, but we reject the notion that God punishes us with suffering. There are, however, ultra-orthodox Jews who blamed the Holocaust on the fact that liberal Jews did not observe the commandments sufficiently. I find this hateful and horrible. We remember how destructive it was when homophobes blamed the AIDS epidemic on the lifestyle of the gay community. I remember how hurtful it was when my daughter was born with a serious congenital birth defect and someone said, "I can't believe that this happened to you," suggesting that I must have done something to cause this suffering for my child. I believe that we must reject the belief in a God that would punish anyone with suffering.

Carla Mae: If God through the Word is going to take on humanness, then suffering is part of the deal. As a Christian this brings up the subject of the Cross for me. Why did Jesus have to die such a death? Was all the suffering necessary? In the Passion, Jesus heals a man of leprosy and in a sense becomes a leper himself. He later becomes covered with our wounds. He warns the man not to tell. But the man just can't hold it in; he goes and tells everybody, "Look, I'm all right, I can re-join society!" As a result Jesus could not go into the town because the leprosy was, in a sense, transferred to him when they embraced. Jesus took the leprosy from him. We understand that suffering is both self-caused and caused by the natural imperfection of creation. Yet we and creation belong to God.

Then because we are God's very own, God joins us there out of love. Suffering attacks God too. God absorbs it, takes the rap for all of us, not just Christians. No one is left out.

Susan: I still wonder why the suffering of the passion was necessary. I understand that there is suffering in the world. I have even encountered God in suffering, but it is hard for me to feel good about a role model who brings about salvation through his own suffering. I also see how comforting this is for the poor and the oppressed who can then find meaning in their own suffering but I would hope that the suffering of the passion was not necessary for the repair of the world.

Carla Mae: As we understand the passion, it is a choice out of love to take on what humans experience and indeed cause. We wreak agony on one another, or it just comes. This doesn't explain why there is suffering. Job didn't really get an answer to that question either. Suffering is simply there, and we really don't know why it is part of the plan. Love comes, not only to join us, to be with us in it, but to reveal to us that it does not have the last word. Life has the last word. The Christ comes bounding out of the tomb like some warrior holding us all, while death collapses helpless. The resurrection is like hope let loose upon a world tortured by violence, sin, and death. The Cross is the symbol of the cesspool that we have created for ourselves. It reveals to us the inhumanity that we are capable of inflicting on one another. The cross is God showing us that God would even go into the dark of death, and show us there is nothing to fear in dying, no matter what someone does to you because God is there too, to bring you out. Death, especially when we inflict it on one another, is the last gasp of egotistical power. It will be defeated by life itself. The cross has meaning only alongside the resurrection. It is telling all humanity that no matter how bad it gets, God will win, and pull us through. We need to be shown this concretely so we will not despair. All of us hang upon our crosses at one time or another. God knew suffering could destroy our faith. The crucified is every man and woman. The risen Christ is every man and woman too. That is God's last word.

Since Vatican II, the church's official position is that Jesus died for all of us. This is an expression of the Word of action and an outpouring of a compassionate God. This mystery of dying and rising was going on before Christianity existed, in preparation among various indigenous peoples in various different forms of religion, but its meaning was not yet understood.

What we are saying, and what the official documents of the Church say, is that no one is outside the range of this mystery, no one. How every person is connected to this mystery is yet for us really to find proper words. In the past there was a very literal interpretation that anyone outside the circle of the water-baptized would be lost. We understand baptism of desire and blood to be more inclusive today. God has obviously been present down through history even prior to Abraham. We've got to look more at this and see the action of God among all peoples, instead of dismissing those on a different path. The language needs to be found. We have always believed that somehow a person becomes related to God or in touch with God through desire. And this is present from the foundation of the world in all different faith traditions.

Susan: We started this series of dialog with *The Disputation*. It is important to remember that we started inviting each other into each other's homes when we were discussing that painful period in history where this very theology was used as a bullying technique. Our conversations are a witness to the possibility of our stories, our garments, evolving and changing. I do totally trust with all my heart that there is a place for me in the world with you. I do not feel judged. I understand that our garments have been twisted and how important our dialogue continues to be.

Carla Mae: I would say more. I would say that for me to be who I am as a Christian, I need you. I cannot be who I am without you, because of what you have said to me. You concretely show me how to walk the talk that I'm talking about. When I say every Christian must be a Christ in the world, I mean that I need to be messianic, I need to be someone who is now going to be the extension of this Christ-person, and this is going to bring about the reign of God like salt or leaven or light. If this becomes real it's going to permeate culture and society. That means it will permeate politics. It will permeate marketing, economics, social work. That means medical decisions. That means healing. That means entertainment. That means purchase orders and commerce and people that are left out or ignored. That has not hit home with many of us Christians. But that's what it means. It means we need to be present in the world and the entire world needs to be salted, leavened, lighted up. It's not some of culture, it's all.

Some extreme Christian groups will say just grin and bear it, the conditions are bad, you're going to have heaven to enjoy later. That is the spiritual valium that some religious leaders use to avoid getting involved with social transformation, social healing, or social justice. They say we just have to put up with it. That's the way the world is. And I'm separate from the world, and I will get my reward in heaven because I have kept myself clean from all that.

Jesus taught us that there are times that we must challenge the status quo even if it does bring suffering. We may even need to go to jail to protest values that are unjust. Many Christians haven't grasped the fullness of what the incarnation means, what the Eucharist means. When they are fed by this Christ they become his extension in the world. A simple answer to your question would be, we have to walk the talk. We have to take the word which has been expressed to us and live it out in that compassionate love that completes the image of God in the world. There's no promise in all of scripture, Christian or otherwise, that I'm going to be successful, that I'm going to totally do this. All it says to me is that I will not be alone in the struggle. But there is a sense here that there is something being formed here that extends through time.

So, going back, we do not believe, for example, in transmigration of souls, because we believe the soul is uniquely created for each individual and is meant for that body alone. Nor do we believe in reincarnation. We do not believe that the soul pops out of the body at death and goes to heaven and then waits to be born in another body and then gets popped back in. We believe that each human being is a totally unique entity and that the soul or spirit of that person is made precisely for that combination of DNA; and it will be as that combination in glory later. It will be in that combination that it is to manifest goodness and compassion in the world and to reach joy and total fulfillment in what we call heaven. Heaven for Christians is distinct, but not necessarily separate from this world. As we sit in this room together, we might want to listen to music. But we are not equipped. If we turned on the transistor that you have, the room would be flooded with music. The music is here, but we don't have access to it. We need the transistor to bring the access. This is heaven. It's a dimension of the real, and we are in it at all times, and what we call the death experience is a moving from this dimension into that dimension by which suddenly we see or experience what has been present all along and we have not had access to it.

Susan: This reminds me of the famous story of the rabbi who wanted to know the difference between heaven and hell. God first takes him to hell and there he sees a grand table set with a feast that would quench every thirst and satisfy every hunger. "Why is this hell?" the rabbi asks. "Look closer," God says. When the rabbis looks, he sees the crooked hands of those sitting at the table, so close, yet unable to feed themselves. "How awful," says the rabbi. "Quick, take me to heaven!" In heaven there is the same table, the same feast, the same participants with the same crooked hands. "Why is this heaven?" "Look closer," replies God. When the rabbi looks, he sees that in heaven the people have fashioned spoons that allow them to feed each other.

Carla Mae: I think the role of religious leadership is to steer people toward an intelligent critique of what they're shown. But I'm under no illusions that because there's been a change of official stance and official teaching in an area that now everybody has suddenly changed their perspective overnight. It takes generations sometimes for people to say "Oh, we used to think that way back then." It's sad to me, and I can assure you I hear how painful it is to you.

Susan: Stories can evolve and change. I remember meeting with a man who came to see me because his marriage was in trouble. He saw that he was a part of the problem, so he changed his life. He changed his work so he would have more time at home; he tried to be more present to his wife and his kids. As we were talking, he said, "You know, the thing I'm most uncomfortable about now that I've done my work, is that it's clear that my wife has a lot of work to do that she hasn't done. I'm very uncomfortable sitting here and saying that it's now all her fault. I know it's not." He said part of his work was to be totally loving and accepting coming from a place of pure compassion. He sensed that if he would say for example, "I've done my work; now it's her turn to do hers," there was something inherently wrong with that.

Carla Mae: Judgment.

Susan: He knew it was wrong. And he was right. What he came asking for, which I thought was so wise, was a spiritual connection that would help him stay in a holy place and nourish his own soul without judging. This desire was a very holy thing. This is what I sense we're talking about. When each of us does our own spiritual work there is hope that the love and compassion we generate will help the other to see the effects of our actions on the other and this will change the stories and reweave the garments that guide us.

Carla Mae: So we have it. You understand what I mean by salvation, and I understand that you don't want to be outside the circle because you do not wear my garment. Our garments take different forms, but the desire of our souls express a common longing for a total human fulfillment and transformation. In this sense salvation is there for us all. I'd say we've begun a new weaving!

CHAPTER THREE

MATTERS OF THE HEART

SEXUALITY, INTIMACY, AND CELIBACY

Susan: This conversation addresses how each of our traditions guides us to deal with sexuality and physical intimacy. As women who have been deeply influenced by the narratives of patriarchal traditions, we recognize the politics of honor and shame that have kept women in their "place" for generations. We also share personal histories of creatively reclaiming and liberating our place and the places of our sisters in both traditions. We acknowledge that women have often had to deny their sexuality to achieve morality and honor in a patriarchal world. For years I have been challenged by feminist scholars I deeply admire who ask how I can be a feminist and serve a patriarchal religion. They even suggest that by doing so I add to the oppression of women. While time will be the ultimate judge, I do feel that my presence and the presence of so many women in roles of authority is beginning to change the paradigm. You and I may look like we are serving in traditional ways, but along with so many others, we are weaving a new gender narrative for the women of our traditions, ancient and modern.

From our conversations it has been quite clear to me that we both value human embodiment very much. We agree that genital sexuality is just one of the many expressions of physical intimacy. Both of our traditions affirm that physical intimacy has the potential to be an expression of holiness.

Carla Mae: First we need to acknowledge that you enter this conversation as a married heterosexual woman, and I enter it as a heterosexual woman who is celibate by choice. We both experience sexuality very differently. A quick conclusion is that I as a celibate do not experience sexuality at all, and this erroneous conclusion is commonly held by a lot of people. We need to search out what perspectives we each bring coming from our traditions and how this perspective colors our own personal approach to the question of sexual intimacy.

The common understanding in our culture today when you say the word sexuality is that you are referring to genital activity. Sexuality is a much broader term identifying the erotic energy of our whole being in its capacity to be creative. We are sexual beings. The way we walk, the way we talk and move, all of this has a sexual dimension. To look on sexuality as equated only with one's genitals is much too narrow. This area of our life is vital and important, and for historical, political and cultural reasons it has often been attached to violence and negativity.

The new paradigm you speak of may be found in understanding compassion or the nature of God, as love; a love that gives itself and explodes into creation. I trace some of my own thinking to Thomas Aquinas who speaks of love as having two movements, two dimensions. One is directed outward because your whole being extends itself when you are in love. Your being extends itself toward the other person. Then there is the movement of delight when you realize you yourself are loved. The two movements are the reaching out and the savoring. Thomas calls it complacency (as in delight) and concern. It is as if this two-fold movement of love was the basis for gender in creation.

In the male genitalia there is the emphasis on outward thrust. In contrast, the emphasis in the way the female is constructed is the active acceptance and delight. Now some might say that's making the female passive, but I don't think so. Think of a nest of baby birds. All the mother bird has to do is land on the bough and those mouths snap open and those little blind birds tingle in expectation. Anybody who would describe this as passive is mistaken. The activity is absolute longing and intense acceptance. This is not passive.

Susan: The Jewish mystical tradition is called *Kabbalah* in Hebrew and comes from the Hebrew root that refers to receiving. It is the received tradition. To receive is never passive. Longing and desire are not passive, and both are necessary for relationship to occur. As human beings we are capable of both, the giving and the receiving and must be free to experience and express both.

Carla Mae: So, in loving, offering and acceptance are the roots of intimacy for me, for both male and female. I see sexual differentiation as created out of the two dimensions of love. When the two reciprocate in sexual union, it is the fullness of love, the coming together. It is a profound way to imagine a God in this union that is both self-giving and accepting in a total act.

Susan: Jewish tradition teaches that the intimacy expressed by a couple on the Sabbath is one of the holiest acts because it replicates the wholeness of God. In our coming together we encourage the coming together of the inner and outer notions of God, the transcendent *Ein Sof* (that without end) and the inner *Shechina,* the imminent indwelling of godliness that makes revelation possible. It recalls how the *Shechina* never abandoned us in exile and will lead us out of exile to be reunited with God, our full potential for *shleimut,* wholeness, that will lead to *Shalom*, peace, for all creation. This act of intimacy, especially on the Sabbath, is the physical reenactment of that in the flesh.

Carla Mae: It's amazing that these deep insights resonate between our two traditions. We see similarities not only in human intimacy, but in the animal and natural realms where the drama is also enacted. We watch it going on, repeating itself as if there is something wanting to be understood so we can honor it. But sexuality is not typically taught that way in our culture.

Susan: This disconnect comes up when I teach our 16-year-olds. It's challenging today because I need to decide how realistic I am going to be with them. I want to tell them that in Judaism genital sexual activity is okay if you are married because you've made this holy commitment to each other. Yet I know that most of them will have some form of intercourse before they are married. I want them to know how precious this experience is. I want them to know that it is an act of replicating divinity and that it is holy. I know that is not the way the culture is treating it.

Contrary to the culture, I tell them they're probably not ready for genital sexual activity. I tell them that no matter what they think, at their age, most of them will not be ready for that level of intimacy for a while. By helping them see it as a holy act, I can tell them that when it is not, they can use and abuse each other. There's a level of maturity that's required for that kind of intimacy that they just don't have yet. However, I do not teach "abstinence only" education because I do not believe that will keep them safe and I do want them to be prepared and know how to be safe. I also believe that it is important for many committed couples to know if they are sexually compatible before they are married. But I can tell them from experience that if they participate in this before they're ready they won't feel the holiness of it. It requires an act of selflessness; a deep sense of what Martin Buber called an "I and Thou" relationship. If it is an "I – it" relationship, then it is utilitarian. A "You-make-me-feel-good" and "I'll-make-you-feel-good" kind of thing can happen without intercourse. This sacred union is different. I will also say that Judaism has always recognized the need for birth control. I've always understood that genital sexual activity is not only to produce children. It's not just for reproduction. For the Jewish community there are times you need to use birth control so that you don't have a baby when you bring that level of intimacy into your relationship.

Carla Mae: For us in the Christian tradition, there is much you have said that is similar to what we believe and teach, but there are also differences. The author Bernard Tyrell writes that those who engage in genital sexuality, in intercourse, in the infatuation stage of erotic love, are condemning themselves to remain there rather than moving deeper into the self-sacrificing love needed for a strong relationship. Infatuation is one of the most electric, the most chemistry-laden, the most physically changing thing that can happen to anyone. It overwhelms you. It changes your whole way of being. You're in love, and so you are different than the way you were yesterday when you were not in love. When a person is in love the endorphin production in the human being is different from when the person is not in love. If there is genital sexual intercourse at that stage, the love has not yet matured to the point where it has the beginnings of the selflessness that is going to make a relationship last. That's why so many times when a couple engages in genital activity prior to marriage, the marriage disintegrates when the infatuation wears off. So what does Tyrell suggest? He writes that pre-marital abstinence in genital sexual activity is not just a prudish idea. It's not just a "You're not supposed to do it because it's wrong." thing. Because there's so much of a sense of wonder in sexual experience for young people this view presents a challenge. A sign that the love is moving into mature self-giving is the capacity to defer gratification, to wait. It's like storing up this wonderful sexual energy so that on the night of the wedding there can be real fireworks!

You say it a different way, Susan. I loved your phrase that if they go too fast and if it's too soon, they will not taste the holiness of it. That's profound. That's really getting at a conviction of mine: I believe that sexuality and religiosity or spirituality, are fused together. I believe that both sexuality and the longing for God are rooted in human desire. The human longs for intimacy with the Holy and with the human. For those who are more academically attuned, I'm talking about the drive in us to actualize pure potentiality. We have the capacity to become more in ways that are phenomenal and transcendent. We long for union. There's something in us that wants fusion. We're made for it. Love is the basis of desire. I think we have a longing for intimacy with the Holy that is the basic longing. Out of that longing for the Holy we also long for intimacy with the human. It reaches upward toward the Holy and then sideward to the human in a communal sense. We need both, and these two forms of intimacy need to be conjoined. If we rip them asunder as we see so often in our culture, we get a promiscuous sexuality that goes whoring. It's looking for union but has lost the sacred context that bespeaks its deepest reality. That's the way I see sexuality and intimacy fitting together from a Catholic Christian theological perspective.

Susan: I would add that one of the things that the sexual liberation movement has brought to this picture is the recognition that a woman's sexuality, her participation, and her pleasure, is important and valued. In fact, the pleasure part of this for both partners is valued in the rabbinic tradition. It is forbidden, for example, for a husband to keep his clothes on during intimacy and it is commanded, depending on his occupation, how often he must bring pleasure to his wife. This is one of the reasons I tell our teenaged students to wait, not necessarily until they are married, but until they are ready. If they are not ready, they're not mature enough to participate in sexual intimacy in the holiest of ways to both give and receive pleasure. We believe that the union of the couple brings wholeness to the universe. It's cosmic. If you don't get it right you could harm the universe in some way. It can hurt the other and it can hurt one's soul.

Carla Mae: Can you say more? How would it harm me or you? If I misuse my sexuality, how would that harm me?

Susan: By not recognizing the holy potential of your own participation in a holy act. Many women believe that their purpose is to please men, so they put their own needs aside. They don't participate wholly in sexual activity in a holy way, and that's not good for the soul. Sexuality and power are often confused. There are cultures where women are blamed for rape and where husbands cannot be convicted of raping their wives. Sex without consent is rape. This dramatic misuse of sexuality is about power not about love. Women who let themselves be used because they are afraid to stop or say no can be spiritually harmed.

Carla Mae: In the Christian spiritual tradition what you just described as the use of another for power, we call *lust*. Everybody understands what we mean by it. Lust is using a person like a Kleenex. You use as long as it suits your purpose and then you dispose of it.

Susan: When you're married to someone for a very long time and you have enough of healthy and holy intimacy, you can sustain some of the times when there are no fireworks and when there's no real sense of the holy. There are times in a marriage the couple doesn't always feel the intensity of the holy. One partner might be sad, and whether you feel like it or not, you let yourself be used for comfort, for the other to feel powerful in the world. You give yourself in that way out of your total love and devotion to this other human being. You want to bring something to the other whether you're into it or not.

Carla Mae: What I hear you saying is that it's a mixture, that it's not always the same, not always the ideal.

Susan: In the real physical world, it's not always what it could be. I think it is safe if in the balance you know the difference. For me holiness in marriage is to have the same capacity for spiritual selflessness. Sometimes out of love you say, "This is not about me. I want to get out of the way. I can be there for you. I know that you'll be there for me when I need it." It is reciprocal even in those times when I don't feel like a "sacred" partner. Our relationships with children, parents and siblings are different. Relationships are all about love. But it's typically only with your sacred partner that you have that vulnerable give and take. This is the mature love that makes a marriage last.

Carla Mae: I treasure your honesty here. This is consistent with what we said about the scripture earlier. It is in the imperfection that we walk our journey, and it is the imperfection that draws love out of us. Not everything is perfect. You don't always have this spiritual experience every time you have sexual intercourse with your partner as a married person. It's just not real.

In regard to my celibate lifestyle, which is looked upon by some as quite odd, how is it that I think sex is wonderful? It's a gift of God. So why don't I enjoy it? When I was teaching undergrads, I was explaining celibacy to a group of freshmen. There was dead silence in the room of some forty young people. One of the students, a young gal in the back of the room, put her hand up. She looked at me and said "Sister, don't you ever think of what you're missing"? It was precious. I laughed out loud and said, "You bet your life!" She was so right-on with her question. The person who is celibate for religious reasons has chosen to be so for a reason. It's not that I just decided one day that I'm not going to engage in genital sexuality. That would be what I'm *not* going to do. But why would I choose to put aside such a wonderful thing? Could it be that I too am *in love* in a different way?

Priests are celibate by disciplinary law right now. Priests could be priests and be married. In the early church they were. It is a disciplinary law enacted in the middle ages, often with very painful stories that continue to be a result of this decision. But with religious communities, the very reason they're together is to share a communal lifestyle committed to other forms of intimacy that are not genital. Witness to something is the very reason for it. The witness is to publicly create a space for God. This is creating a deliberate emptiness as a sign in culture for a space for the holy. If a person is going to enter a religious community, the question has to be faced: How are you going to use your sexual energy, because it's there. You don't leave it out on the doorstep when you enter the monastery or the religious community. That's nonsense. Each one of us is a sexual being.

In the past, before we became more at ease in talking about human sexuality, we took for granted that those entering could just "grin and bear" it. There was little or no positive guidance in how to direct sexual energy in a healthy way. It was taken for granted that you would learn to manage as you lived the lifestyle. We were coming out of a somewhat shame mentality regarding physical intimacy. In renewed Catholic communities this is no longer true. Authentic Catholicity celebrates the physical with great joy. Joy in creation is the base of our sacramental emphasis. We use water, wine, incense, oil, bread, vestments, music, art, and all of nature in worship. The Catholic community is quite sensual along with the Orthodox, Episcopal and Lutheran communities. These are the sacramental traditions. We are not Puritan in the sense of being suspicious of sensory experience as obstructing one's union with God.

Susan: You mean these more Puritan communities fear physicality instead of understanding the physical as a vessel for the holy?

Carla Mae: Yes, as understanding the physical as an actual window to the holy.

By the early centuries in the Christian community there was the conviction that a life totally focused on the quest for holiness was doing so using the same erotic energy that is manifest in genital activity in marriage. It was simply being focused in another way. There was an intuitive sense that these two energies, the desire for union with God and the desire for deep erotic sexual expression or energy are really bonded together. If the person was going to be fixated on the pursuit of God, one had to decide about that erotic energy. A person can certainly be religious and be sexually active. There's no question about that. But if you're going to make the pursuit of God the obsession of your life, becoming so absorbing that you are concentrating your energy on it, then this is a distinctive call. In one sense you become unmarriageable. This is the charism or gift of virginity in the early church. The sexual energy is totally focused on God and the pursuit of union with the holy becomes so all-consuming that it dwarfs other relationships.

As I understand it, as Jews view this, such a condition is unusual and is only deliberately asked by God to make a point, as in the case of Ezekiel who was told he was not to weep when his wife dies. He was told he had a job to fulfill and he needed to be totally absorbed in it. In the early church those called to this were considered "married" to this obsession. All their energy was so focused on this pursuit that they would not seek genital pleasure and comfort in an earthly partner. They fasted from genital sexual experience for the sake of their pursuit of God.

Susan: This is not foreign to our tradition. Moses tells the "men" not to go near a woman at Sinai in preparation for receiving the commandments. There are fast days when we are supposed to refrain from physical intimacy so we can focus on the sanctity of the day. But there is no sustained celibacy in Judaism. In fact, desire is celebrated. Denying that can lead to corruption.

Carla Mae: That's why I go back to that early beginning. Celibacy as a distinct call from God has no meaning today if it's simply legislated without the call. If a young woman would come to me and talk about entering religious life, I would not really start with asking, "Are you capable of selfless service? Are you interested in living in a community of women no matter what your orientation, whether you're heterosexual or homosexual.? Are you going to be able to build your relationships mainly with these women and be content?" I wouldn't start there. These questions are very important but if you're going to embrace this lifestyle for religious reasons, the desire to pursue intimacy with God must come first. So the question becomes, "Is the pursuit of a relationship with the Holy going to be your primary intimacy? Can it be the center jewel of your life, surrounded by the setting of all your other relationships?

Susan: You describe celibacy as a part of your spiritual practice, like yoga or meditation.

Carla Mae: More than a part, it's a permanent, freely chosen, openness. It's a radical poverty. It's similar to what happens when an artist forgets to eat because he is so taken with what he's trying to express through artistic expression. That's similar to what I'm trying to say. But it's also true in a sense of the married who are celibate except for that one person. There is also a disciplining of the sexual desire in marriage.

Susan: Yes, there is.

Carla Mae: You have to know *who you belong to*, you have to know *whose* you are.

As part of their training today, candidates for religious life need to examine all of this to make an informed commitment. They don't make a commitment permanently in the beginning because this is a type of lifestyle that you really need to try out. For the married this is where a long enough engagement is important so that the compatibility can be tested. The woman or man considering religious community has approximately six to nine years in what we call temporary commitment. They make a temporary commitment and at the end of that period of time they examine it. This is a deeply prayerful thing.

Susan: And if they choose to leave it's not seen as a failure?

Carla Mae: Not anymore. It was in the past. But today there's much more of an understanding of a search, of trying to find your call, trying to find the lifestyle that's going to give life to you so that you can be fruitful in a very different way.

Susan: So, there's not necessarily the opinion that you are more spiritual if you are celibate?

Carla Mae: Formerly in the Church's history you had to be in a religious role of some kind to be considered spiritual at all. In this older view those who were religious, or priests were considered more spiritual than those who were married.

Today the official Church recognizes that what makes a person more spiritual is the love they bring to their lifestyle, whatever it is. There are going to be people in various parts of the Catholic world with different degrees of understanding this. But what changed all of this officially was Vatican II. The Council described a universal call to holiness. From this it is clear that everybody on the face of the earth is called to holiness, to union with the divine. The love that brings about this union measures the depths of spirituality, in whatever lifestyle. The lifestyle is where this universal call is lived out.

It is clear from your question that you are very aware that not all people have made that transition. Official position or not, you will have within the Church those who still want a type of pedestal treatment because that's really why they entered priesthood or that's why they entered religious life. They want deference shown to them. When they realize holiness is not automatic, that it's their love in the lifestyle that makes one holy, some leave.

Susan: If it was a choice of giving up something to get something back, then it's not going to work. You can't just give up genital sexual experience because you think you're going to get something back on the outside. It has to be an offering, almost like a sacrifice to God, with the understanding that it will deepen your relationship with God.

Carla Mae: Yes, because it really is a form of fasting. It's choosing to remain empty so that something can come in and choosing to do this in the name of the whole human community. It is a lifestyle that deliberately and publicly creates space for God.

The only reason that fasting is healthy is that it helps you to get a sense of proportion in your life. When it's about fasting from food, it puts your intake of food in proportion. It makes sure you are not so obsessed with feeding yourself that there is never any space in your life for the Divine. It's a very symbolic act, to restrain your intake of food in order to create space spiritually. It can be a very profound experience. Celibacy is related to that.

Susan: One of the ways I connect with what you've said is our own fast days. Fasting is more than not eating. We can learn about fasting from the story of Esther. Before Esther approached the king to plead for her people's lives, she fasted. She fasted because she needed to create a space in her that would draw God into the story to make room for God to change the heart of the king.

Carla Mae: If I remember correctly, all her maidservants fasted with her, in sackcloth, and prostrating themselves.

Susan: This teaches us that when many fast at the same we make space and draw God into that space. I think that's why communities can pray and make a difference. They make that space. We have both seen that collective prayer really makes a difference.

Carla Mae: You hit on something when you used the word "sacrificial" to describe the motivation. This is very important. Being faithful does not come from gritting your teeth and feeling tough. The faithfulness does not come from power. It comes from emptiness. You need to be filled with something else and then you are satisfied. No one can understand what I'm saying unless you've been there. God knows the needs you have as a woman. You don't leave those needs outside when you come in the convent door. When you consecrate your entire life to the service of God you are empty because you're not going to seek the comfort that would come from a genital union. So you fast in that area of your life. You sit there with your emptiness and beg God to fill you, and more, to fill the world. Dedicated celibacy is not a private matter. It has a social dimension. You become like a "landing space" for God, giving the Divine a place. The decision gives voice to Psalm 63: "I thirst for you, I long for you, more than a dry and parched land without water." Such a vowed person becomes a beggar. Rather than the elite church lady seeking pedestal treatment or deference, the person in consecrated life becomes the beggar who makes a space for God. When it is genuine, people know it when they see it. They knew it in Mother Theresa. Everyone knew that she was filled with that emptiness, that space. It was as if she had enough room and compassion for everyone.

It's like the reed that the shepherd carves out from a branch. If it is not emptied out and then pierced to make the finger holes, there will be no music. There is no space for the breath to come through. The celibate lifestyle is counter cultural. It doesn't make sense unless this deep dimension is there. Those who have made that choice need to keep making it each day. A married woman does this too, day after day, if she is faithful.

Susan: That is so true. In my case we've been married forty years and I can tell you that one does make sacrifices, make choices, and find ways to recommit oneself and fall in love again. You learn to look deeper into yourself and into the other person. It is also a spiritual practice to love the same person again and again, in so many ways. You don't always stay in love in the same way over the years.

I have seen this with many couples. When things get difficult many tend to want to walk away and say this wasn't meant to be. Sometimes it wasn't meant to be because there's abuse. Sometimes there's so much damage done that as broken human beings they aren't capable of forgiveness. But some know that it is going to be hard going into it and they are brave. They really talk about everything from money to sex to housecleaning, to all the big things that are going to be hard for them. They're not getting married with any illusion. It might be the hardest thing they've ever done. It's like dancing. It's easy to dance alone. I have these theories about the generation that invented these alone dances. It's different when you dance together. It's hard. It takes practice. It can be messy and you often find that you are a little out of sync. You step on each other's toes.

Carla Mae: One of my dearest memories is to see my mother and my father dancing together at their golden wedding. They had been through such horrendous things together. But there they were, cheek-to-cheek and dancing, just feeling the rhythm of each other, after fifty years of struggle. Remembering that picture is such a profound experience for me that very often I recall it when I pray.

I think the married lifestyle is also a communal lifestyle. You build community with this person and then the children come. I am convinced the most challenging lifestyle is the single lifestyle. The single person has to be very intentional about who their primary community is going to be. They don't have a structured primary community as married folks do, or those in a communal lifestyle. They have to be much more intentional about identifying the communal aspect of their lives, or what will support their living out of their loving.

I'm convinced you don't get your rank or your worth primarily because you're in this lifestyle or that lifestyle. You are who you are by the amount of loving you are able to do. The lifestyle that is the most suitable for you to do that, that draws everything out of you, that allows you to interrelate, and to follow your deepest heart's desire is where you need to be. You become whole and holy when your intimacy needs have been met by knowing someone deeply and being known by them. Intimacy takes many forms. Genital expression is one form. I believe this discussion could bring all of us a deeper understanding of the role of sexual expression in our lives, when it is a proper expression of intimacy and when it's not.

Susan: I believe that this conversation is another example of how our new garment weaves together and values the diversity of our expression and affirms that the common thread, when we speak about intimacy in relationship, is love.

Sexual Orientation and Gender Identity

Susan: I would like to begin this conversation by offering an understanding of redemption as the opposite of exile. We know about exile. The Torah is our guide to end exile by expanding the circle. We are taught to "love the stranger," again and again. Everyone was present at Sinai, from the one who draws the water to the one who chops the wood, from the leaders to the marginalized, even the unborn. In fact, Jewish tradition teaches that Torah was given in the ownerless wilderness that it too would not be owned, and its universal teachings would one day level the playing field and end exile for everyone. I believe that this requires us to keep the door open for everyone who wants to be in the circle and desires to serve in holy ways and to be an accepted part of the community. This lays the groundwork for including everyone regardless of sexual orientation or non-binary gender identity.

Carla Mae: The Catholic Christian community frowns on homosexual activity and at the same time demands respect for the homosexual person. I must live within my tradition at the point to which it has come, but I do need to address how the homosexual person is to love. In the writings of the Catholic

Church homosexual activity is considered a disordering of human nature. But in the context of being called out of exile, being called out of rejection, the Catholic community needs to hear the challenge of an opening to change the notion of a disordering and to embrace a more inclusive view. I enter this discussion with that listening in mind, while trying to respect my Church's concerns.

Susan: I believe that we have misinterpreted the Biblical laws about sexual expression between two men. It says in Leviticus that two men shouldn't lie together. This is in the context of many teachings including one that says that a woman should not wear a man's clothing. The prohibition stands within the context of a greater teaching that is about respecting one's nature or orientation. So, if your orientation is to be heterosexual, the scripture is referring to you, because it's promiscuous to go against your nature. If your orientation is to be male, be male. If your orientation is to be female, be female. If you are transgender, be transgender. If your orientation is to be heterosexual or homosexual, or bi-sexual, respect your orientation.

If you are transgendered, then we'd better help you feel comfortable and accepted, also, because God made us all. The teaching is about respecting one's inner identity. If your calling is to come to your religiosity through a call to celibacy, then that's your orientation. If your calling is to come to your spiritual connection to godliness through marriage, honor your path. I do think there are boundaries. I think it's in finding those boundaries in our communities that we identify ourselves. Our challenge is to figure out a way to really listen to each other and make space for each other's different orientations, to treat each other with love and to fill the spaces between us with holiness. This is my liberal Jewish interpretation, but I am far from alone in believing that sexual orientation is not a disorder or a choice but the honest expression of one's identity and one's nature and this must be honored and accepted if we are to end exile and reach toward true redemption.

Carla Mae: If one's orientation is not a mistake and science is able to confirm this, then we may need to rethink what we have said in the light of this new understanding. I would hope that the Church would be open to the facts that come to us from science that help us understand better how a human being is constructed. It is also important to acknowledge that this is not just a Jewish or Christian question, it is a human and global one. In some cultures, the homosexual is revered as a shaman or holy person in the community. These men and women in their abstinence or celibacy, maintain a respected position in the community as a pointer to the holy. From our discussion on celibacy you know that I believe that people who model the expression of non-genital love can provide an important depth and diversity to a society that is often obsessed with sexuality in unhealthy ways.

Susan: If individuals choose celibacy in the ways that you have described, that is one thing, but to impose it on a whole genre of human beings because they are gay is beyond cruel. You are right to suggest that this inclusivity in the religious community is challenging. One of the core values we shared in forming our congregation was to make a safe place for people who were left outside the circle. This included Jews by choice, intermarried families, Jews of color, and certainly the GLBT community. Many felt that they had to check their queer identity at the door before they entered. We wanted to create a community where everyone was welcome not only because they are human beings created in God's image but also because we could not be whole without the presence of the GLBT community. This was challenging because the Jewish and the larger social communities were particularly homophobic in the early 1980's because of the AIDS epidemic. We had to do many things to create a safe space. We had to change the hetero-centric books and materials in our school.

We had to make sure that we had openly gay role models for our children. We had to tell people not to join if they were uncomfortable with gay couples showing affection in the same way that we are used to seeing straight couples. Having clear principles helped us create a culture that was welcoming and safe within a larger community that was not comfortable with these behaviors.

Carla Mae: I think that this discussion is vital and requires both justice and compassion for these brothers and sisters. It also calls for education. We need to continue to learn how to respond through prayer and dialogue and by listening to science as it unfolds. If sexual orientation is rooted in the very design of a human being and is not a choice, then we must acknowledge it. It has been the stand of the Church to require celibate loving of those who are not heterosexual. As we have discussed, celibacy does not limit love and intimacy in one's life, but it finds genital sex inappropriate.

I think the Church's position comes from the conviction that genital sexual activity has a distinct two-fold purpose. It is to provide joy and comfort to the partner, and by its very nature be open to new life. That "new life" is usually interpreted to mean *biological* life. This would mean that a sterile partner, although labeled as such, could still be genitally active, because the "openness" is there, even though it can't be fruitful. In other words, there is no obstacle put in the way of the sexual expression. This also means that one can sin with another without any contact whatever, because in one's imagination, there has been full genital expression.

The challenge before us, as I see it, is to discuss with LGBT persons what real intimacy is for those whose body parts don't "fit together" in order to produce biological new life. What is, in their view, a holy way to be intimate according to their nature? Does it mean being genitally celibate by choice to be true to their physicality, and yet very creative and authentic? Is genital sex activity being foisted on LGBT persons in imitation of heterosexual persons? What does it mean for them to be true to themselves?

Pope Francis, in my view, has been a breath of fresh air in his October 2020 comment that LGBTQ couples deserve the legal protection of a civil union contract. This speaks compassion. It says nothing about marriage, as the Church regards marriage as between a man and a woman.

Susan: I have had to council many couples with children when one of the partners finally acknowledges that he or she is gay and there is often much pain and confusion. I long for the day when people do not have to fight their nature for fear of rejection, judgment, exclusion and even hate crimes. I believe that this non-acceptance comes from ignorance and that it adds to the violence of the world. You have taught me that celibacy can be a holy choice, but it needs to be a choice not a mandate imposed upon a group of people by a community. I have learned from the GLBT community that there is a spectrum of gender that includes many wonderful people who are transgendered who have also been marginalized and victims of violence as well. It seems cruel to label people as deviant for being true to who they are, for being true to one's nature. I hope that our new garment will have threads of acceptance for all of us no matter where we are on the gender spectrum and that our sexual identity does not keep us from having the kind of loving, meaningful and intimate relationships we spoke about in the last chapter.

FOUR

LIFE'S BEGINNINGS, THE SOUL, AND CERTITUDE

Carla Mae: The source of all life is the Divine Mystery. Human life is derived from that Divine Mystery as it comes from God's word shaping it through God's Spirit hovering over the chaos as is shown to us in scripture. This is the way the Christian views the text.

Our role as the offspring, or as the created reality from that Divine Word, is to become wise or become knowledgeable about the very process by which that takes place. Science is unfolding this wonder to us. This scientific data is itself in the Mystery we call God. Science is not opposed to this Mystery. It opens a secret, a marvelous becoming that has gone on from the beginning. We live it from day to day in the sacred context of human relationship. We have not known much of its wonder in the past. But now, as science unfolds this to us and can really give us the details of how cell division starts at conception, we marvel at the electrical exchange and the energy that make it work. Why does that electric exchange work? What is the life force behind the electricity itself, triggering it? We wonder about what causes the attraction of the sperm to that ovum and the penetration of the ovum. What is working there? What is the dynamic of the life-giving energy-power that is working, and what is our role in that? Is it to assist and to somehow cooperate? Is it to stop the process? Is it to turn it off? What is our role? And where does arrogance come in, which we recognize too readily as being part of both of our traditions? Arrogance turns the divine into the idolatry of human control. It allows the ego to believe it is in charge and in this case decide on matters of life and death. We know this propensity exists within the human, but I think it's not clear where the arrogance line is crossed, and we start playing god.

Susan: I agree that we must guard against arrogance, but I also see that the very nature of creation presents us with difficult choices. For example, let's consider an ectopic pregnancy, where the egg and the sperm that have united to create a potential human life implants in the fallopian tube. If it is allowed to grow it will kill the woman. You could take the fertilized egg out and put it into someone else if the highest good is to preserve that division of cells, but in Judaism, we would not risk the life of the mother to save what is considered, at that point, a potential life. Judaism teaches that our ability to study and learn from science is a gift from God and we are meant to be co-creators with God in the repair of creation. We have teachings about when life begins, and when the soul enters the fertilized egg, but we also recognize that this is something that we cannot "know" definitively. Believing that we can know is the 'sin of certitude.'

Carla Mae: What you bring up for me, Susan, is the further reflection on the whole dynamic of creation. We see how one thing sacrifices itself for another constantly. This dynamic is present in the whole pattern of creation, even in the change of one species and the disappearance of another. The fact that one species feeds off another even in the microbiological realm is for me with my sacramental perspective, a constant form of communion in the religious sense. It is a type of communion by which one substance gives of itself to another, and then goes out of existence for that substance to live. But that level of discussion is something those of us in sacramental traditions can wrestle with. We are working here within the constructs and the mental frameworks that have guided our moral decision-making down through the centuries. What I would call this more eschatological or cosmological theological discussion is a new topic and would indeed be challenging for us. To look at the way creation continues, and the way that there is self-sacrifice or self-donation in that very process is profound. That this self-giving is captured for us in the human sexual act is amazing. We are the only species as far as we know who think while we are engaged sexually, and the self-emptying, the self-gift, the sacrifice, or the offering, the vulnerability of one person to the other as they engage in sexual intercourse is unique to us. Learning this points to a distinctly human and intentional spiritual function, a higher or transcendent level that relates to other levels of life in the entire cosmos.

This self-sacrificial offering is revealed in the disappearance of a star in its collapse to produce what happens in a supernova. It is the elements being transformed one into the other by a form of death, by a form of self-giving. If we fail to ponder this wider view, and see only in a very narrow way, then our viewpoint is quite confined. I speak here from a spirituality perspective. The only way that we can really guide that process in an ethical way would be out of an immense self-sacrificing love. And that is something neither you nor I nor anyone can guarantee in those who are the players on the stage. The only way that it could be almost guaranteed that there would be ethical sensitivity in the movement of such self-giving love would be with scientists who have a total respect for the two realms, both scientific and sacred. It is as though we would invite them to come into our world of self-giving love, and to do their science from within that world. I don't think it's wrong to wish and hope for that, but I think that some of them find the religious world to be ridiculous because it is not based on empirical data. They operate from a set of principles that are purely pragmatic and confined. In staying within a purely secular worldview there is the human potential of desecration because the possibility of a transcendent realm is denied.

Susan: I cannot agree that people who don't use God language or go to the church or the synagogue or the mosque can't be as good and as committed to doing God's work as anyone else. In fact, in my experience, it's those very scientists that can be the most spiritual people, especially in the area of the embryonic stem cell debate. It is those scientists who have the greatest awe for the immenseness, and the deepest humility for what they have in their hands every day than anybody I've met in this whole arena, including the politicians and the religionists. It's the scientists that are coming from the holiest place on this.

Carla Mae: I agree that this indeed can be so. I'm not saying that mere religious talk solves this. It is the openness to what we know as a religious set of values that keeps us from putting quick boundaries on human activity and falling into premature certitude. What you are describing is an integral and whole authenticity on the part of these scientists. What you are talking about is a person who is really aware of the depths of the ramifications of what he or she is doing. I don't mean that the language has to be my language or your language, because we all know there are those who speak the language and who don't live the words. We certainly want to give the full benefit of the doubt to people who come from that authenticity. My concern is with those who want to impose their limited secular view on people of faith. Can the law in any way guarantee that authenticity? Or does that come from an inner resource and openness that the law has no power to demand?

It may be helpful at this point to discuss "the soul" as we understand it. For me, coming from my Catholic tradition, very much influenced by the scholar Thomas Aquinas, the soul is a *life force*. As a created life force, it has no being of itself. It draws existence from the One who *is*. Remove the divine, and the soul falls back into nothingness. In other words, it's a created *potentiality*, a dynamism of possibility, always becoming more and more itself. It has distinct operations and works within matter causing development and growth.

There is nothing to "pop in" or "pop out" of a body. For us as Catholics, souls are not prefabbed, stored up in some heaven, ready to pop into a cell cluster when the blastocyst gets to a certain stage of fetal development. Rather it is the *dynamic life force which causes the development in the first place.* We believe that this dynamism is created instantaneously, at the moment of conception, for each individual, and then begins the orchestration of its development according to the DNA given it. If the genetic structure is inadequate, the life force works with what it has been given. There is no magic wand making it all right.

This life force is made to work with matter. Without it, the soul has nothing for its energy to work on. But it is not limited to matter. Coming from the Divine Mystery, it has *spiritual* functions as well as biological ones. The life force that is the soul orchestrates the formation and development of the physical organism with its various systems: the circulatory, the neurological, the digestive, etc. It is rather new to be thinking of the soul as actually causing the physical development of a child. We usually think of the soul as just "there." But it is dynamic. It makes the potential *actual.* This view brings with it clear ramifications on terminating this activity at any stage. It raises the question of crossing the line and interfering with the direct action of the divine as the source of the energy itself, which is a form of blasphemy, the height of human arrogance.

The "soul-energy" or "psychic energy" then mutates and orchestrates the affective and emotional operations of the human psyche. The empirical operations at this level are the human's image-making capacity, dreaming, fantasizing, imagining and its eleven powerful emotions. This number comes from Aristotle, and Thomas understood the wisdom in the Greek's analysis.

The emotive motors or passions come in two sets: the *spontaneous* emotions, and the more *considered* emotions. The spontaneous emotions are six: love/hate, desire/aversion, and joy/sorrow. They are rooted in the physicality, are more connected with sensate feeling, and spring up spontaneously when we are stimulated by sensate interaction. The considered emotions are five: fear/courage, hope/despair (impotence), and anger. Anger has no opposite. It responds with the urge to fight or to flee. These powerful emotions are subconscious for most of us unless we attend to them and bring them into our conscious awareness to address them. This is the stuff of what is called "mental" or emotional health. Psychic energy in this form is the field for the psychologist or psychiatrist and is a rather new discipline.

Finally, there are the operations of what we might call the upper part of the soul. These operations can also be empirically observed. They open us up to transcendence, to that which is beyond the physical and the psychic. They are spiritual operations, unique to human consciousness in the development evolution has shaped to this point in human development.

First, there is wonder, and we can be aware that we are awestruck. This is the basis for the worship of that which is beyond our smallness. We *attend to our experience* with a self-reflexive consciousness. We can observe ourselves silently wondering at the beauty of someone, or something. Then we begin to *question*. We can intend to question. We can attend to our questioning, and know we are doing it. Next, we can *arrive at a tentative conclusion or judgment as to the facts* we have arrived at by our questioning. Finally, we weigh the worth of what we have learned, and *decide what we intend to do* about it. The empirical steps of what we have called the spiritual capacity of our intelligence and free will, are quite clear:

1. Attend to your experience
2. Intelligently question
3. Arrive at a careful judgment
4. Act on what you judge to be of most value to help heal the world.

This path, the orchestration of physical development, the psychic-emotional development, and the unfolding of the cognition and free choice – these are operations of the human life-force or soul, if Aquinas and others are accurate. This no "pop in" bubble waiting for a new body to inhabit.

Susan: One way to frame a Jewish understanding of the soul is with her three names. The Hebrew names for the soul are, nefesh, ruach and neshama. This allows us to speak about our metaphor of the garment that expresses the body, the body that holds the soul and the Soul of the soul. As with most theological ideas, there are many divergent opinions on the nature of the soul in Judaism. However, all opinions agree that in this life, the body and the soul are one. Assuming that we can know the nature of this mystery can lead to the sin of certitude. But, we have our beliefs. I believe that when one dies, the soul leaves the body and is eternal. I recognize that this is a belief that gives me comfort and guides my decisions. The Soul of the soul is God and is found within us when we are alive. When we die, our souls return to the Oneness that is God. The levels of soul that have been imprinted with the uniqueness of each person, allow us to feel the presence of those who have died. I suppose one could say it is like the light of a star that we see and can even feel long after that light has gone.

I'm not sure what I believe about souls that return. I would like to believe that the separation between worlds is something we cannot understand while we are in this life. A wonderful rabbi, Naomi Levy, wrote a brilliant book called *Einstein and the Rabbi.* Her book is a guide to the awareness of one's soul. In it she describes Albert Einstein's response to a rabbi whose young son died while he was caring for the children who survived the Buchenwald concentration camp. The grieving rabbi asked Einstein if he was to believe that there was "nothing within his beautiful young son that has defied the grave and transcended the power of death?" Einstein replied, "A human being is part of the whole, called by us 'Universe,' a part limited by time and space. He experiences himself, his thoughts, and feelings as something separate from the rest—a kind of optical delusion of his consciousness. This striving to free oneself from this delusion is the one issue of true religion. Not to nourish the delusion but to try to overcome it is the way to reach the attainable measure of peace of mind." As a rabbi who has buried more loved ones than I can count and as a mother who has lost a child, I find comfort in Einstein's words.

The conversation on the nature of the soul leads us to ask how we live with our deep differences when it comes to beliefs that determine what is morally acceptable. If the Church believes that life begins at the moment of conception, then the Church must be against abortion and the methods of birth control that cause spontaneous abortion. The Jewish tradition is clear about the mother's life coming first and does not support your notion of self-sacrifice as a holy response. In the way I interpret and understand my religious tradition and teachings, we have a very different understanding about birth control and abortion. In my tradition I have clear guidelines for when birth control is permitted and when abortion is permitted, and they do conflict with the teachings of the Catholic Church. How do we politically live together? How do we make space for each other when our religious traditions really guide us to respond in very different ways to the same situation?

Carla Mae: I really think that the first step is a basic honesty. If we speak in such a way as to compromise our own traditions, then we are not honest. First, I can tell you what the Church's position is today and how it is commonly interpreted. Then I can expand on that, and that is what I did above in sharing the theology behind the Church's teaching by referring to Thomas Aquinas. What is so very important to me is to understand that each of our traditions reaches a judgment regarding the facts of something because of the data that we have and how we understand it. We can only work the way that humans work and the way they think things through conscientiously and with care. This is working from the data that we have. If we ever think we know it all we are in danger of falling into unwarranted certitude. Certitude is stopping too soon with too little. Faith humbly acknowledges that we are not all knowing, we are not God. We are moving together into the Mystery, and as we do so we can hold hands and tell each other what we have come to in our exploration.

I'm going to just bounce back briefly to the days of Galileo. First, a clarification on what really went on. The Church was not against Galileo's theory that the sun was the center of the universe. The Jesuits were suggesting the same thing at the time. The problem was that the instruments were not sufficiently developed to prove it. The Church asked Galileo to teach it as a theory. He agreed to do so until the facts were in. Then he published and went back on his promise. He taught the theory as a *fact*. The censure was on this betrayal, not on the science.

The Church was operating out of the data that it had, that it thought was the truth at that point, and was trying to be true to that in what it said. It has recently come to a point of apology because now we have more data which has dramatically changed our beliefs and our actions. Another example of changed data is bloodletting. Physicians thought that if you caused a person to bleed it would help them get well, and so they would inflict the wounds so that the blood would flow and that would be considered a cure or a help. They were going by the knowledge they had.

To me, the basic honesty of saying that even in our moral positions we need to humbly admit that this is the best we can do at this point with the knowledge that we have, is important. If we take the posture that our beliefs are final, and our wording is going to last forever, then there is nothing more to learn from you or from the scientists or from anyone else. I think this is lapsing into the arrogance that we have been trying to shake off since the beginning of history. As a Catholic community of faith, we need to learn that even our doctrinal positions must expand in meaning with the data that comes from the sciences with each passing age. This in no way is denying their truth. It is the constant challenge to deepen our own synthesis of that data along with our religious position and move it further if we need to. This is a valid stance of the Church. We believe that there is a development of doctrine or dogma. This means that a truth can deepen and expand, and the human mind comprehends more and more of the truth as wisdom grows. The thoughtful person rarely says outright, "You're wrong." The human process of coming to truth and knowledge is a discursive one. We move from questioning to fuller comprehension. We begin with initial data, then question how the data fits together, and then come to a tentative conclusion. And why is it tentative? Because if you get more data you're back to square one, starting to ask more questions and integrate that data into judgment that may make previous judgments and conclusions deepen and expand.

Susan: I totally resonate with what you're saying. The sin of certitude is when we think we have the answer for all time. Instead we can make space for compassion and mercy to guide us, recognizing that there's a very good chance that our ideas will grow and change as they have throughout the ages. If there's a situation where I have to make a difficult decision, instead of making a fence around it, because this is what I know today, my tendency would be to leave room and make a judgment on relieving suffering. So if it's a child pregnant by a rape, or a woman pregnant with a pregnancy that's going to put her life at risk, because I don't know some of the answers there, I would err on the side of compassion. This is the best we can do today. Something happens in the womb where ensoulment or potentiality for human life begins. I do not believe that we know when or how that happens today. We have beliefs about this, but we don't know. But what if we find that out in the future? I think for me there must be humility. For me now, in this situation, it means that we choose compassion for the life that we know, and not the unknown, and this allows for the termination of a pregnancy when the mother determines that her life is at risk.

Carla Mae: I would add that there needs to be total honesty to the data before us, the data that comes from revelation and from science. Another point on which we agree would be humility. The careful guarding of humility, of a non-arrogant openness so that I can listen to what you are saying and what you hold in great value. As you say to me that you would prefer a space rather than a fence in the cognitive judgment on the truth of this is new. Until now, women's voices on this have not been heard.

What you are proposing, and what I would support, would be this constant type of dialog so that we can call one another to deeper insight. If a space is kept open so that we don't shut down too quickly on our inquiry, on our honest questioning, and on our honest listening to each other, then it is possible for us all to win.

This posture is symbolized so powerfully in the burning bush narrative that is so familiar to both of us. Moses does not understand the phenomenon that he is approaching. He takes off his sandals, his protection, so that he can be connected to the earth and be vulnerable. He assumes a posture of humility before what he does not know.

I don't see that very often in my own Catholic community. I think it's a real disadvantage for us. It causes us to miss the basic nature of the church, as a *listening* church. We are very intent on being a *teaching* church, and yet our own documents call us to listen deeply before we speak. We influence best by sharing with the people who are in our community, and those who are not, the truth we've arrived at to this point; that would be honesty in giving them moral guidance.

I long to hear from my own Catholic community the humility of wanting to learn from others, of being willing to learn, to listen. This is a basic quality of the church that we find in many of our ancient writings, that first of all, the Church is a listening church and then it is a teaching church. What is common to us both here is the fact that we need to assume a posture of listening, and then we proclaim the truth of our convictions. We proclaim the truth of what we know or what has been our experience, what has been revealed to us as we presently understand it. That first posture of reverent listening before the other, whether it's Jewish or Islamic or the Eastern traditions, reveres a divine activity. The divine activity may be different than I have experienced, but who am I to say that God is not present in the religious searches of other people? In saying that, I would be going against some of our own documents. I need to listen for the divine working in religious searchers very different from me. I have only begun to see that being done in a really serious way.

A public openness to this kind of listening has been the Assisi type prayer where John Paul II invited all the religions of the world to pray with him at Assisi. There the leader of the Catholic community assumed a posture of listening to the prayer of all of these different peoples. It was a stance that the head of the Church took publicly in front of everybody. He received immense criticism from some within the Church for doing so, even from some of the cardinals. I think that what John Paul was claiming was that the listening identity of the Church is core to its identity. In much of what we're discussing, I understand that my community is in need of constant conversion. I see my Catholic community as growing into true universal catholicity only when it goes through the depth of that constant *converto*, that constant conversion. An arrogance or resistance to the Spirit of God moving within any community, ours, yours, anyone's, is unworthy of us as seekers after God. We must be ready to take off those sandals. And that's a frightening thing because the sandals of my thought, the sandals of my conclusions, my constructs, whatever my mind has come to, those sandals protect me as I walk on the sharp stones of the journey. And so, to take off my sandals I leave myself defenseless, because my tender feet are going to have to be exposed to something I may not be familiar with, and this is the listening posture that I believe is so vital to the contemplative soul of the Church as it moves into its presence in the world. Without that humility, the Church can come off as arrogant and as non-compassionate. It can fall into the "sin of certitude." This is a posture of protecting a frozen dogma, rather than rejoicing in a vibrant revelation that challenges and gives life and joy.

Susan: If our beliefs and our doctrines become so absolute, so certain, they do not leave space for the listening. We betray the very essence of serving God. This can happen to anyone of us because it is human nature to want that certainty. Our traditions are meant to help us be better, in this case, to listen deeper. Do you remember a Thursday night in October of 2006 when religious leaders from many different traditions from east and west gathered at a Catholic Church on the Feast of St. Francis and prayed for peace, each from our own religious traditions? It was the second-to-last game of the World Series and my husband could not believe that I was dragging him away to participate in the service. We were also leaving our daughter at home who had been waiting for a heart transplant for a year and a half and was running out of time. Most people stayed home to watch the game that night, but the clergy showed up. I know that we were all praying for world peace, but I could also feel that the clergy, many of whom we had known for so many years, were also praying for our daughter. I listened to each one and felt the holiness, the Soul of the soul, making room for something more. The next morning, we got the call that there was a heart for her and that night she had a successful heart transplant (and the Cardinals won the World Series!)

I believe that the relationship we have built over the years of listening brought us together and created that opportunity to make room for each other and our differences in a most loving way.

We were listening without an agenda. Often, we begin with the end; we start with where we want to get to, which is our own truth. What I have learned in dialog with you is that I have to let go of the end if I'm really going to listen and hear what you have to say. I have to be willing to move from wherever I may be stuck, wherever I may seem certain about anything, I have to be willing to be flexible, even to change, to be in real dialog.

Carla Mae: You are articulating exactly the process that I was trying to describe when I said you begin with an experience, and a listening, you ask questions, you begin to put "A" together with "B," and you come then to a judgment that you couldn't have reached if you hadn't done those steps. I think our lack of understanding of how this process works can result in our becoming defensive. If we say we have come to the truth and we have not paid attention to *how* we have come to the truth, then what is to preserve us from a very biased view of what we are calling the truth?

Susan: In that case, should religious faith inform or guide social policy and politicians in a democratic society that's composed of people with different religious convictions and traditions? What responsibility does a religious tradition that finds itself at odds with American culture and political will have, to be open to the truths of others? Let's take Roe vs. Wade, for example. Some in the Catholic Church have taken a very firm stand on Roe vs. Wade and would love to see it overturned.

What if it is shown that attitudes and opinions that come from the pulpit are seen to encourage a Catholic citizen to take it into his or her hands to stop abortion by shooting a doctor who works at a clinic where abortions are performed. This happened to one physician who was lighting his Sabbath candles on Friday night when he came home from the synagogue. Someone shot into his kitchen and killed him. What responsibility in a pluralistic society does one religion have when it takes such a firm stand and then its congregants act on it in a way that really can be destructive to society?

Carla Mae: First, it is important to say that there are Catholics who are opposed to the reversal of Roe vs. Wade because they fear the return of back-alley abortionists. From the documents that I have read, the Church's position would be totally against the violence that has been shown by extremist Catholics or anyone else. It is also true that the Catholic Church has been very public in opposition at abortion clinics. But the Catholic Church would be totally opposed to anyone using violence as a tool to meet an end however good that end seemed to them. The end does not justify the means and that is a basic tenet within Catholic law. At the same time, we can only understand this behavior if we understand that abortion to the Catholic is a form of blasphemy. It is telling God that we will engage in the activity you have designed for us, but we don't want the results built into it.

Susan: We can say that and yet, knowing human nature, the certainty of this teaching always has the potential to bring out this potential for violence. What responsibility do we have when our teachings cause people to be extremists?

Carla Mae: We are fully responsible for what we say from the pulpit. We cannot condone killing to show that killing is wrong. Making it even more sensitive, if there would not be the legalization of medical abortion when desired by women, what is the alternative for women who do not share the Catholic conviction that human life begins with conception? What is the morality of going back to the back-alley abortions and having women start to appear again in emergency rooms where they are going to die because of botched self-mutilation? If medical abortion is totally outlawed, which was the condition before Roe vs. Wade, does it really solve the problem to reverse it? These are honest questions that need to be asked.

I think the dialog today very slowly is beginning to go, not so much in an either/or position, but that both need to go beyond the present impasse: abortion on demand versus no abortion under any circumstances. There needs to be real discussion on this question, recognizing that the issue is broader than just the termination of a pregnancy. The issue has to do with a total societal condition regarding the rights of women as well as the rights of the unborn. The woman is not just a baby-machine, to be impregnated at the whim of a partner. She is a temple of life. The role of the Church is to midwife an intelligent and compassionate discussion, without an ironclad agenda already in place. There needs to be the space created for this honest discussion without penalty.

In the past, a person like Rembert Weakland, the former Archbishop of Milwaukee, began such a discussion. He had an open discussion with women who had abortions, to share stories so that he could hear all the reasons and experiences that brought them to their decisions. He was soundly criticized for this and looked upon as a wildly liberal bishop. This was a truly missed opportunity for the Church. It could have moved the dialog from the heat of how furious people are to the point of churning up violence, to the point of really trying to understand the agony that brings a woman to choose to have an abortion. When we as Catholics say we don't need to hear those reasons, we stop being a listening church.

The role of the community, Catholic or otherwise, is to foster the type of dialog that will not just simply create a short-term solution, legal or illegal, but to work for a broader and much more effective solution that is not just going to be shortsighted and pragmatic but is going to really influence the structures of people's lives. This dialogue needs to be open to the principles underlying belief and practice.

Susan: When there is room for dialog there is hope that we will be able to help society provide the right framework for women to make the holiest decisions. If we take away fear and guilt and shame, we may make room for a more honest conversation about family planning and reproductive rights. A Hebrew play on words teaches that the "*mei siach*" which translates to the 'sea of dialog' in Hebrew will bring the "*Meshiach*," the time of the 'Messiah,' a time when all are heard and valued for who they are.

Carla Mae: Another difficult conversation around right to life issues was brought up by the Terri Schiavo case. She was a young woman kept on life support even though she was in a persistent vegetative state after massive brain damage. In that case we saw a conflict even within the Catholic community on the issue of preserving human life. The Church has said that that tube should not have been removed from Terri Schiavo, that she should have been sustained and that removing it was an active act of euthanasia. The question for me is the use of extraordinary means. It is one thing to use life support measures on someone who has a chance to recover but to insert a feeding tube when she was already in a vegetative state or in a condition by which there was no reversal, is to me questionable. In my opinion, it was probably an unfortunate decision to have inserted that tube in the first place. At that point she could have been made comfortable and been monitored so that the natural processes in her body could have quietly taken place. I believe that is the compassionate thing to do. Human biological life is good. We value it highly. But for the Catholic community it is the prelude to another kind of life, and death becomes a kind of birth. It is a form of violence to insist that a person "stay here with us" when it is clear that death is immanent.

Susan: I agree with you and I very much see it that way. At that moment when they had to make a decision to insert that feeding tube, I'll bet there was still hope in her loved one's hearts that there would be a miracle. In the beginning I imagine that there was still hope that somehow those brain cells would recover because there is so much we don't know. We're in such a grey area. It's the grey matter of the brain. We think we know about the brain stems, and the top of the brain, and the side of the brain, and the right brain and the left brain. There is much we do know from theory but we are just in the infantile stages of science really in many cases being able to tell us. I still agree with you that with what they knew at that time, if they could have been a little less attached to her in their lives and more attached to what was best for her, they may have been able to let her go. It took fifteen years and a terrible court battle to let her go. But it is not often completely clear what to do. When I'm called into Children's Hospital and people are trying to decide whether or not to put a child on a respirator, we ask if the respirator is going to breathe for the child just long enough so that it gives the child a chance to rest and regain his or her strength, or is the respirator just going to prolong death? But it's not always that clear. So, we have to give ourselves an out at some point, and that is what finally happened with this case.

Carla Mae: In light of all that, once that tube was inserted, I think they should have let it be and not have removed it. Yet in removing it, I can understand that there were those convinced it was the most compassionate thing to do.

Susan: In Missouri, the law says that once you put that feeding tube in it's really hard to take it out. In traditional Judaism we don't "fluff a pillow" if it will hasten death. But we are also not to get in the way of God's will. There is a strong belief in traditional Judaism that every moment of a person's life, regardless of what we would call "quality," has meaning. Someone in a vegetative state, for example, can still be a presence for loved ones and I have heard it said, can still pray. I have seen this taken to extremes when suffering is prolonged. I cannot support this.

Carla Mae: My father died in 1989 and there was no living will or power of attorney. My father had open heart surgery and had to have his infected sternum removed. He never recovered consciousness and was on dialysis regularly. My two brothers, who are both businessmen and are very different from their sister the theologian, sat down together with me. We called the doctors in and asked what our father's potential was for recovery. They looked at us and they said two percent. We said, okay, then why is he on dialysis? They shrugged their shoulders. We asked what would happen if we took him off the respirator? They said he would suffocate. After asking all our questions, we agreed that what we needed to do at that point was to help him die in the most dignified and comfortable manner possible. That became the agenda, to let him die the most peaceful, humane death medicine could give him and us. We stood around that bed, one by one removing all of those extraordinary means and were with him as he slipped off into eternity. We moved like three dancers in synchronized movements. But it was not active killing. It was simply removing extraordinary means and letting nature just unfold the way it was headed anyway, and so we kept removing the obstacles that would have forced him to remain.

It was a remarkable experience. It was painful, but the unity, the communion between my brothers and myself took us beyond ourselves to a place that was the best thing for our father. We felt totally one in our love for him and in our care. There was no division at all. If there would have been, it would have torn me apart. We were not educated in all of these technicalities. But we were guided by love what to do and what not to do.

Susan: We can learn much from your experience. I also hope that families are encouraged to have these difficult conversations before they need to make such difficult decisions. I encourage everyone I can to have a health care directive and a living will.

Carla Mae: This reminds us that we are partners in this whole life process of living and breathing, of life and death. Our challenge is to partner in this immense mystery and in the drama of life and death without arrogance, without this pompous know-it-all attitude of power. Can we, with dignity and with calm peace, deal with the limitations and the imperfection of both our knowledge and our capacity to choose from that knowledge? That humility is key when we are talking about these most difficult subjects. In my tradition the metaphor of humility is washing feet. An arrogant person cannot wash feet.

A final word on what we believe happens to the soul in death. If the soul is a "life force" of the body, then death is the loss of the life force. The body then begins to deteriorate because there is nothing there to continue to animate it. So where is the life force? Where is the soul? One view is that the sin of the world, its arrogance, destroyed our relationship with God. Without that relationship, the created life-force would die at the point of death along with the body. But God never intended that. God intended that life force to be a part of God's own being, the One who is life itself. The person needed to mature, to become all it could be and then would be caught up to God from whom its life-force had come. Somehow the break that the sin had caused had to be mended. The friendship relationship had to be restored. Then the divine plan of eternal life with God could once more be realized.

This is where Jesus comes in. God comes in person, "God with us," to mend the break. In the person of the eternal Word, that Word presses itself to human DNA, thus effecting a marriage that can never be dissolved. God did the restoring by uniting God's own Word to the lost one, breathing into the human again the breath of eternal life. This is what the resurrection is all about. It's not just about the human Jesus. It's about us. All of us are restored. Even those who don't know it, and who may not want to know it. In transforming that human DNA, God gives a preview of our future, the future of the whole human family. This doesn't depend on believing it. It rests in God. We will perhaps learn it by experience one day, no matter where we stand religiously. Again, we need to be open to the possibility. It is all about a new life, a life that can never die.

Susan: Perhaps it is in that humble space of admitting that we cannot know with certainty that we can find the threads to weave a garment of compassion and cooperation when it comes to the difficult issues of when life begins and when it should end.

Understanding the Sin of Certitude

Carla Mae: In the New Testament (Luke 6:36) Jesus asks if it is wise to sew a new patch on an old garment. He warns that doing so would ruin the garment because the strength of the patch would tear the old fabric. Are we attempting to do that, Susan? Are we falling into the *sin of certitude*? What does your tradition have to say about the "other?" How do we stand for something yet avoid the pitfall of a false certitude?

Susan: Rosh Hashanah is so much easier than Yom Kippur. On Rosh Hashanah I can talk about the opening of the tent and believe that collectively we generate enough good to overcome any evil inclination. Together we lift each other's spirits and believe that the kindness and compassion and justice in the tent will continue to nudge the story of humankind to a higher and better place. The possibility of being part of the holy community of the tent strengthens our faith, inspires us to do more and I have seen it save lives. The outer reality of the community inspires a greater inner spirit for the individual. But the work of Yom Kippur is inner. On Yom Kippur each of us is called to do our own personal work so that the inner individual spirit can influence the outer reality of community. This is much harder work.

The metaphor for Rosh Hashanah is the tent but the dwelling for Yom Kippur is the *mishkan*, from the Hebrew word *shochen*, "indwelling of god." *Shechinah* comes from the same root. The tent gives us infinite possibilities for *tikkun*, repair, of the broken world. The *mishkan* gives us the promise that no matter how difficult life is there is also hope for a bruised or broken soul to heal and have joy. But the Yom Kippur liturgy does not focus on how good we are. The prayers and teachings for this day are about sin. There can be no Yom Kippur without sin and there can be no final turning, no redemption without Yom Kippur. We invite the sinners to stand with us for the *Kol Nidre* prayer that we offer on the eve of Yom Kippur. On Yom Kippur even a *tzaddik,* a completely righteous person, must admit that they may make vows that they cannot keep and repent and turn in their ways. In the Talmud it says a fast where there are no sinners present is no fast. In the mix of the incense in the temple that we would burn to draw godliness into the holy space, there was always one spice that had a bitter smell. Without this ingredient, which represents the bitter smell of the sinner, forgiveness and redemption are not possible.

There is no original sin "doctrine" in Judaism. But we all have a *yetser*, the inclination we have that gets us into trouble. We get lazy and miss the mark, we get greedy and take what isn't ours, we break promises, we are indifferent, we hurt intentionally. We do too little or too much. Sin comes in many forms. Yom Kippur comes to teach us that when we face our sins and name them and atone by intending never to repeat them, we prove that we humans have the power to change, to remake ourselves and be renewed and reborn.

We learn about ultimate sin at the climax of our story in the Torah at Sinai. At Sinai, when we are just about to receive the Torah, the great reward for the *chutzpah* of leaving slavery behind, we sin. The greatest sin in the Torah is the sin of the golden calf. Cain killing Abel, Jacob tricking Esau, Joseph's brothers selling him out, these were big sins but not as big as the golden calf. (For Jews Eve and the apple was a good thing, inside the garden we had no purpose, outside the garden our lives had meaning but that's another talk.) It wasn't the calf itself, or the gold that made it such a great sin. It was a sin because we fashioned the calf. We didn't believe that Moses would come down from the mountain. We were too attached to Moses and lost our faith in ourselves and in God. We were scared, we wanted something familiar, and something we could see. We turned to a golden calf that represented all that we had worked so hard to leave behind. With the calf we betrayed the promise that tomorrow could be better for ourselves and our children. With the calf we stopped believing that we could change. The calf represented the good old days that really were not so good but kept us in the comfort zone of what we knew. It was a feel-good materialistic and simplistic answer to the threats around us and kept us from having to face the much greater challenge of being a free people, each of us with a responsibility not just to ourselves but to a greater whole. The calf made us slaves again; it required only fear and obedience. It could not love us back and it couldn't care if we loved each other. It represented everything evil we had left behind but with Moses gone, our world seemed to be crumbling around us physically, spiritually, and morally. It was so hard waiting, not knowing what would come next and so we turned to the golden calf even though it meant giving up our hard-earned freedom. We turned to the calf because we were afraid for ourselves and our children. Without Moses, there was more stealing, adultery and violence. Without Moses, the courts were backed up. So, instead of controlling our *yetser,* believing that the good in us could win, we gave ourselves over to the cynicism of the golden calf that said that only fear could control us and only money and power and self-interest would motivate us. In the moment we were sure that Moses would never return and we needed something we could see and know and be certain of to hold onto even if it meant giving up our freedom and our hope for a better life in the promised land.

Carla Mae: Are you saying that making that calf was trying to find *certitude*? Was it trying to sew their new situation onto an old yearning for security? Was it the sin of making something "other" an idol?

Susan: The golden calf is so filled with itself there is no room for anything but itself. No room for a new thought or a new idea. The sin of the golden calf is the sin of certitude, believing that we can know what we cannot know, losing all humility, and from this sin, despite Moses' pleas for forgiveness, many of us die. We learn that the price for false certitude is great.

I have seen the sin of certitude up close many times. I remember that at the end of a legislative session in Jefferson City, the senators were hearing testimony about stem cell research.

It was very late. Supporters and opponents of a bill to criminalize stem cell research had been testifying for hours. I listened as the sides took turns addressing the senate committee. Everyone was so tired. The more vocal senators kept asking the same question, when does human life begin? Is this destroying a life, a human life, they wanted to know. It was my turn to speak. Just about everything had been said. I decided to testify anyway because we were told that the numbers of people speaking against the bill that would criminalize stem cell research would matter. I looked at their tired faces through my tired eyes and I told them about a woman who had just died. I had just been with her and her sisters and I told her not to be afraid. I told her that I believed with all my heart that she would find her way from this world to the next and find her way into her mother's arms. I could see the senators nodding their heads in agreement. But then I told them that these are my beliefs. Of course, I believe them, but they are not something that I can know. I told them that they were struggling to know things that we just do not know. They were struggling to make decisions based on a certitude that is just not available to us, except in the inner space of our faith and as they struggled to know what they cannot know, people are suffering, and dying of diseases that this science could cure.

This, for me, is the sin of certitude. Like the golden calf, the sin of certitude reduces the complex nature of creation to a single simple response that leaves no room for interpretation. The sin of certitude is what keeps us from tempering passion with compassion. It is what allows the fanatic who opposes abortion because they believe it is murder to murder those who work in the clinics. The sin of certitude also has room for only one idea. It is what keeps us from listening to alternative views with open minds to receive new information and ideas that could change our beliefs not for political or self- serving reasons but because our hearts have opened to possible new truth.

There is a beautiful image in the Jewish tradition that describes the kind of religious sensibility that the Talmud tries to nurture to save us from the sin of certitude. It says, "make yourself a heart of many rooms and bring into it the words of the house of Shammai and the House of Hillel, the ones who declare clean and the ones who declare unclean." Judaism says, become a person in whom different opinions can reside together in the very depths of your soul. Become a religious person who can live with ambiguity, who can feel religious conviction and passion without the need for simplicity and absolute certitude. We have many examples of this in our tradition. In our collective heart of many rooms lives the belief that one must not fluff a pillow or touch a dying person if it would hasten death and the belief that if there is an obstacle that prevents the departure of the soul such as a noise or salt present on the tongue we must stop the noise and remove the salt to allow for the death. We have been there together when in one moment we are praying for healing and in the next we know it's time to let go.

To counter the sin of certitude, we try to produce souls who are not afraid to interpret situations in multiple ways and offer arguments for different positions and points of view with a kind of humility that always remembers that this is the human point of view and not God's. Political and religious leaders and Supreme Court judges who lose this humility put us all at risk.

The sin of certitude always limits us and keeps us from the wonder and the promise of the possibilities for healing and hope in our *mishkan*. The calf tells us that we must conform to the crowd, that we must be invisible to be safe. The *mishkan* tells us that each individual has something unique to be valued, that each of us with our own gifts must be fully present, visible, on the front line for the *tikkun* to occur.

The calf tells us that we need to be *certain* to commit to a relationship or a goal and that questioning, and doubt are weakness. With the golden calf we see a frozen reflection of what is, and we become attached to it even if it is no longer true or good for us. We are trapped in the certitude that this is the only way, the only solution, the only path and we cling to it even when it isn't right for us anymore. The *mishkan* always leaves the space for doubt and possibility; it allows us to take risks that will grow into greater love, greater opportunity.

With the calf there is no room for change, so we create
stories that keep us from having to change, to grow, to do
the hard work that living demands. Then we desperately
need to believe them even when they are no longer true. The
mishkan reveals the complex nature of our relationships, of
society and of creation and gives us a way to live with the
ambiguity. We do not have to pretend to be certain when
we are not. We do not have to pretend to know when we
don't, and we can let go of the stories that keep us bound
to the idolatry of the calf, to stories that keep us stuck. We
reclaim the possibility of change and transformation. There
is no room for *teshuvah* in the calf; *teshuvah* only exists in
the space of the *mishkan*.

Another example of how we can resist the sin of
certitude is with Israel. The space in the *mishkan* of our
hearts allows us to love Israel without having to believe
that God is an instrument and a guarantor of our political
and nationalist success. The sin of certitude leads us to say
that the land belongs only to us, but the *mishkan* teaches
us that what matters is the present. In the present we are
dwelling in a dynamic relationship with the Holy that
demands that there must be justice in the present. The
torah teaches that we must have one law for the citizen and
the stranger, understanding that our stories, and the way
that we interpret our lives, would be different from those

we share the land with. The *mishkan* teaches us that we cannot cling to old stories or messianic aspirations, but we must live in the present. Only in the present reality will we recognize that the heart of many rooms requires all sides to give up the certitude that only they will win. All will have a place, or none will. The *mishkan* gives us the hope that a new solution will emerge.

Whether we are talking about stem cells, or choice, or assisted suicide, or the future of Israel, or the many genocides that have occurred since the Holocaust, or the earthquakes, or storms, or floods occurring from the climate crisis, or lack of affordable health care, or racism, or homophobia, the sin of certitude threatens to keep us from responding in holy ways.

With each one we could find a problem that would give us an excuse not to respond. "It's too complicated, it's too hard, someone else is doing it, I'm not completely sure, it's too messy...." With each one we could fashion a golden calf that leaves no room inside for us and people would continue to suffer. Or we can embrace the *mishkan* and leave room for the possibility that each of us could be a small part of the solution.

I know that it's difficult living with uncertainty in our inner *mishkan*. It's difficult when you are waiting for chemo to work, for healing, for a child, for love. Some days it feels impossible to live in between the spaces of the uncertainty. We long to fill it with certitude even if we must lie to ourselves.

Surrounding the story of the golden calf are the instructions of building the *mishkan*, the tabernacle. The *mishkan* is the antidote to our attraction to idolatry. The Midrash says that it was on Yom Kippur that we first heard the words, "make me a mishkan that I may dwell among you." "Make ME the mishkan," the Holy One says, teaching us that any place that godliness dwells is dynamic. Any place godliness dwells requires relationship and different possibilities and opinions. The contrast to the solid calf is the openness of the *mishkan*. Like our tent, our inner *mishkan* has room for us and for godliness and for something we have not even imagined yet to emerge. The very first time that the word forgiveness or pardon appears in the torah is in the story of the golden calf. We say, *v'salachta la-avoneinu ul-cha-tah-teinu* : forgive our iniquity and our sin (Ex 34:9). Standing together, standing with the sinners and the righteous, opening the inner sanctuary of our hearts, guided by compassion, leaving room for something new, we chose life for ourselves and our children and grow and nourish the souls that guarantee that from our big and wonderful tent blessings will continue to flow.

Carla Mae: What I hear in what you are saying, Susan, is that certitude blocks us off from making room for the "other." It prevents making room for the "other" as part of a genuine solution. The real solution needs to bring the "other" inside the circle instead of locking them out and to create a garment where there is no other.

Susan: In our new garment, everyone must have infinite worth and there cannot be any tolerance for de-humanizing anyone. In our new garment we must also deconstruct racism in both of our histories and traditions.

FIVE.

FACING THE
LEGACY OF RACISM

BEYOND NEW PATCHES
ON OLD GARMENTS

Susan: We are both white women who believe that we must support the Black Lives Matter movement if we are to weave a garment that will celebrate the infinite worth of everyone and include, honor and respect diversity. We are inheritors of the Doctrine of Discovery that justified Christian and Western domination and superiority and justified colonialization. As people with white skin we must also root out of our own systems and souls the legacy of White Supremacy that allowed for the transatlantic slave trade and has built systemic racism into the very fabric of this nation. We live in a city named for

Louis IX, a Crusader who burnt thousands of precious Jewish books and participated in the plundering of Jewish, Muslim and Eastern Christian communities to fund a world order that would favor white Christian Europeans over all others. We live under the cloud of the Dred Scott decision of 1857, when an enslaved African American man unsuccessfully sued for his freedom and the freedom of his wife and two daughters. It was no accident that our racially divided city of St. Louis, became the site for the Ferguson Uprising of 2014.

Carla Mae: I came to St. Louis in the summer of 1986. I had a lot to learn. My first impression in watching the evening news was amazement of the generosity shown in the city. Folks were bringing box fans to certain locations to give to others who had no air-conditioning in the midst of a hot summer. But I have learned. I learned about the facts you speak of above, Susan. I learned of the race-riots of the 60's and of white-flight. I learned that St. Louis had over 90 suburbs, little municipalities that used profiling and traffic stops of people of color to fund their budgets. I learned of the one stubborn rabbi who remained in a city torn by racial strife. It took a while, but I soon met that rabbi in person, and a relationship grew that found us looking squarely at the facts above and a lot of other facts. Among them was the difficult Jewish/Christian dialogue which was our focus for some time. But you led the way with the chronic racism that was embedded in St. Louis.

Susan: I am part of the black lives matter movement that was born in Ferguson in 2014 when 18-year-old Mike Brown was killed and his body lay out in the hot sun for four and a half hours as his mother stood by and could not hold her son as he bled out into the street in front of her. I had been showing up for years protesting gun and police violence and with the only synagogue in the city limits earned my place with clergy fighting for racial justice. The day Mike was killed was a tipping point.

A scab was torn off a deep wound that day and when social media sent those images out we all knew that something had changed. The clergy had to come out into the streets, the police were going to be held accountable, and the divides between the two Fergusons, the two St. Louis's and the two Americas were no longer going to be tolerated, because the marginalized, the vulnerable and the oppressed were demanding a place at the table. We who could not stand to see another mother's child die, were determined to make that awful moment a movement that would bring about change. And we would not let that wound be covered up until it was healed.

A young man in our congregation knew Michael Brown. Had he not been at the synagogue on the Saturday afternoon Mike was shot, he could have been caught in the crossfire that day. He is a young Jew of color and has been taught to keep his head down, not to run from police, to expect to be stopped for no reason and to not to have an attitude.

This is personal for the Jewish community because these are our children, this is our community and to be a Jew is to be part of the solution, not part of the problem. Jews know what it is to be marginalized. Our work is to move the margins to the center.

In St. Louis, the racism and the violence that we are seeing has been waiting to erupt for decades. Tax bases, property values and self-interest have created the institutional structures of oppression that have added to the economic and racial segregation of our neighborhoods. Ferguson, Missouri is not the inner city, it is a pleasant middle class suburb with shopping centers and Starbucks. Many families moved to Ferguson to give their children a better environment. But the profiling by the primarily white police of the majority African-American population was bound to cause problems.

Racism in America is a poison that is stealing the hope of many for a better future. The events in Ferguson shine a harsh light on this reality. It is part of a broader picture about the need for hope and opportunity for our young people. There are just not enough jobs that provide a living wage. In Ferguson, we see the fragility of a middle class that is one crisis away from falling through the cracks.

This disparity of class has caused us to have two Americas because it divides us and keeps us from having personal connections across the divide.

So, with distrust in the legal system already flying high, we reached beyond the tipping point that has brought more and more people demanding change. We hope that after years of white flight and economic disparity and a lot of talk, maybe this time, because of the engagement and fervor of the community, because of the energized young people who have found their voices, there will finally be justice for all the Michael Browns and a change to business as usual.

When the media left, the protestors moved on and the businesses were restored on the main streets of Ferguson we knew that our work had just begun. Today, the next generation has been awakened and empowered but so have the white supremacists and white nationalists who unleashed the racism, anti-Semitism, islamophobia and homophobia that are further dividing us and threatening our lives.

We have joined with clergy of all religions who have left the safety of our buildings and have taken our ministries to the streets. The congregation that I helped to found almost forty years ago was created to be a presence in the urban core where the ravages of racism and economic disparity are visible through the windows of our sanctuary. We have worked to end the violence of the poverty cycle by being in the center of the fights for making health care accessible to all, more restrictive gun legislation, equity in education and immigration reform. We are leaders in the Fair Food Movement that demands an end to the modern day slavery of farm workers, fast food workers and others who work full time and do not make a living wage that can lift them out of poverty. We are able to be on the front line of this movement because we have worked hard to dismantle our own internal racism and have made a place for Jews of all colors and our interfaith allies to listen to each other, to learn from each other and to work for justice together.

Carla Mae: In my early years at Aquinas Institute of Theology I was in charge of a program for folks very experienced in ministry coming for sabbatical time. As I was coming to know the city, I realized how important it was for these sabbatical priests and religious to come to know what had happened here too. I contacted a black historian named Billie Crumpton. I explained that I wanted to take these sabbatical people on a tour, a tour from a black perspective. She contacted a driver with a van, and for the next few years, this tour was a highlight of their sabbatical time. When I asked Billie to tell me her impression of the Catholic leadership in St. Louis regarding the racial question, I held my breath. Surprisingly, she said that in her view it was quite positive. There had been solid integration efforts on the part of the Catholic bishops. I learned of the efforts of religious women in education and health care. Fuller information would come later as I learned of the deep racial tension hidden, but festering like an unresolved infection in the Catholic community.

Susan: Racism and all forms of hatred can be fatal in the hands of extremists and in the hands of some police in an America still not having come to terms with a racial divide that puts all of us at risk. The Torah tries to teach us that this separation is ultimately illusion. In Genesis chapters 21 and 22 we learn that if we are willing to sacrifice the child of Hagar, (in Hebrew, *Ha-ger*, the stranger,) in the very next chapter we will be sacrificing our own children, as Abraham nearly does to Isaac.

It's also important for us to understand that the legacy of slavery has built a conspiracy of shame that dehumanizes people of color and sets us up to blame the victims. The "thug" language that was used to distract us from mourning the lives of teens like Mike Brown and Von Derrit Myers and Trayvon Martin, and even twelve-year old Tamir Rice needs to be seen for what it is. A shaming of the victim to get people in power off the hook for perpetuating systems of oppression. Shame gets inside and becomes what we call internalized oppression. But we heard loud and clear a new generation, a generation the baby boomers told that their lives mattered, calling "look at me!" The young protesters linked arms in the face of the police in the early days of the movement and they continue to this day as they shout, "When you see me see a nurse and a mother and a student and a human being like you." They were rejecting the shame meant to control them.

While we were still protesting the shooting of Mike Brown, another teen was shot by an off duty police officer. Carla Mae and I were both there at the site of the shooting as protestors gathered. I saw the mother of the young man standing in shock, her son's blood still on the ground. She turned to me and said, "Don't let them turn my son into a thug."

The challenge is to turn these critical and often, crises, moments that get our attention into a movement that does not just birth band aid programs as a response to suffering but sees that we need systemic policy changes that get to the root causes of the suffering. We are being called to transform a nation that has been built on the backs of slaves to one that truly does see and value the infinite worth and the godliness of everyone, absolutely everyone regardless of the color of their skin.

I see this as an opportunity for the Jewish community to see the great opportunities and responsibilities we have when we are no longer wanderers but the stewards of the land, both as American Jews here and in our relationship with Israel. In this new chapter of the civil rights movement often referred to as the Movement for Black Lives, (a movement that embraces the words *black lives matter* because there are so many black and brown lives that do not matter as much as much as white lives,) we are called to dismantle the systems of oppression that have built racism into our everyday lives. Racism is so the norm that people with skin privilege do not always see it.

As with many of you, I see the disparities everywhere and for the sake of the black Jews in my community, my black neighbors and friends, truly for the sake of everyone, I continue to work on the agenda that has been part of the many platforms put forth again and again since the 60's lead by SNCC and the Black Panthers and yes, even the Reform Movement of Judaism. None of this is new, but we must keep telling ourselves that just because, Dr. King and Rabbi Heschel marched together, we do not have a place at the table today. The new and exciting circles of leadership that include queer people and women are interested in the relationships of today not yesterday. And, yes, the not so new agenda includes the connections made between the colonial transnational oppression of people of color and the plight of the Palestinians. We need to be able to converse intelligently about how Israel, like all other modern nations suffers from an entanglement with the effects of empire building upon indigenous people who become oppressed and invisible, like the Palestinians. Add to this the parallel but separate narrative of a persecuted ethnic minority, the Jews, that culminates in genocide of the Holocaust and you get a people who does not forget our vulnerability no matter how much state power or privilege we have. You get what we have today with an unwillingness to give up power and privilege, even for peace. Who could blame us.

It should be no surprise to Jews that the Ferguson to Palestine connection was part of the black liberation agenda and, more specifically, found its way into one paragraph in the Platform put out by the M4BL's after Ferguson. I became a kind of poster child for what happens to Jews who dare to be part of the BLM movement, do not support BDS or buy into the critique of "normalization" and call themselves progressive Zionists. I became a "real life terrorist" locally and a two headed cartoon monster internationally. I was called out as, "Progressive except for Palestine." There was no room for and/ and. The choice put before me was either/ or and it really was no surprise. I was an easy target because I was out there on the street, in the protests, getting arrested. The attacks were serious but the support from my friends in the movement because of the relationships of trust that had been built over more than thirty years of showing up was much louder than the critique. Also, I would not let the attacks distract me from the work, or from continuing to be on the front line. I remain committed to being an ally and holding the space for my black protestor friends whose lives are at risk every day, **every day,** because of the color of their skin.

I do this because it is the right thing to do and I want to be on the right side of history, on the side of the oppressed.

I do this because when I am present in the work I will not be made a token, a "good" Jew who takes sides against Israel. Being present forces the confrontation with the oversimplification of Israel and Palestine and it forces the conversation that challenges the demonization of Israel. I have found that when I listen I leave space for others to ask, what is my relationship to Israel? What does Zionism mean to me and how do I understand the occupation? Do

I believe that co-existence is possible? When I am present when these questions are asked, I am more likely to offer a more nuanced response.

In these conversations I do my best to tease out the stereotypes that feed anti-Semitism. Just as I have learned to identify racist red flags it is important for us to intelligently call out anti-Semitic rhetoric and assumptions. I experience again and again, a perceived power imbalance. Many people, good people see Jews in America and Israel as the people with the power. These dynamics feed a tendency to dehumanize us partly because many really don't believe that they can hurt us. We Jews on the other hand see ourselves as a people and a nation at risk. Just look at our story, and little Israel in the midst of a hugely hostile middle east. We see ourselves as vulnerable.

I will continue to teach and preach that Israel has the right to exist, that Palestinians have a right to self-determination and dignity and that supporting these narratives is what it means to be pro-peace. And I believe with all my heart that we can build the relationships of trust, and be part of the solution. This can be a crossroads moment when identities do not have to compete, and we can weave a new garment of our entangled histories with compassion.

Carla Mae: I'm in awe of your front-line presence through these years, Susan. Your voice has been steady and brave, and I'm glad that its story now is written here. My own direction has taken another turn, due to some extent that I have been a faculty member of a graduate Institute. Because I'm linked to the Institute, I need to keep clear when and how I can appear on the front line. My name is connected to the Institute, and I can't assume my personal stands speak for everyone there. So I work more behind the scenes, through the Workers' Rights Board of Jobs for Justice, for example.

Most of all, my energy has been focused on your final phrases above: "...we can weave a new garment of our entangled histories with compassion." Back in 2009 I heard Karen Armstrong present the Charter for Compassion at the Melbourne Parliament of World Religions. I brought the possibility of making St. Louis a City of Compassion home with me, and presented this possibility to David Mehl, then the Director of Interfaith Partnership. We contacted Louisville, KY and a visit there resulted in Louisville mentoring St. Louis in the early stages of becoming a compassionate city.

I saw this effort as an under-the-radar campaign for attitudinal change for the entire region. The Charter for Compassion was like a Trojan Horse. Who would be against compassion? Yet if enough organizations and individuals signed on to the Charter, posted it so their feet could be held to the fire, and we could hold 'shout out' Town Hall Meetings to cheer on those living by the inclusiveness called for in the Charter, we might just begin to get at the deeply engrained racism that was still poisoning the St. Louis Region.

Our first Town Hall Gatherings focused on those who had been on the front lines in Ferguson, and those involved in the Report that followed. But we were clear from the start: Interfaith Partnership which had birthed Compassionate STL had to move the effort into the civic community. After a lull period following the retirement of David Mehl, leadership fell to me to take CSTL in this direction. With a Core Team of folks faithful through this time, we worked out a ten-year Vision Strategy with the help of Joe Reagan, formerly from Louisville, but now in St. Louis. We connected with the national Charter for Compassion Office in Washington state for our finances. We built a website and Facebook outreach, and started what we knew would be a long-haul. Our final goal is to get St. Louis onto the Realtors' Index of the 10 most compassionate cities in the US where you would want to live. Being in the Heartland of the United States, and yet having cardiac arrest, we realize is no small task. But with a growing list of Partner organizations and individuals (we're at about 130), we hope to keep growing this Base and slowly heal this long-held racist divide.

The pandemic has strangely been an aide to this goal. It has brought to the surface our national festering racism, no longer cloaked by indifference and denial. It will be hidden no longer. The work has just begun, Susan...you on the front line, and me hidden in the Trojan Horse, waiting while the city sleeps to release compassion in every area of education, medicine, sports, communication, law and law enforcement, city government and services, entertainment and the arts. We need to make the Ferguson Report a reality. We need to recover from the Civil War vestiges that still haunt us as a former Slave State. From the outside and the inside, we need to weave equity and compassion into our new garment.

CHAPTER SIX

WOMEN IN MINISTRY

OUR STORIES

Susan: In the Jewish mystical tradition, Sarah stands at the opening of the tent. She stands in the breech, not in or out. She keeps the tent open to possibility, to creativity, and to something new. I might have been named Sarah in another generation but my parents, the children of immigrants, wanted their children to fit into the American culture that had rescued their parents from the Holocaust. I was named for my fathers' mother, Sarika, (the Sephardic version of Sarah) so I became one of the many granddaughters who would have American names that began with an 's.' In just a generation, we felt safe enough, perhaps assimilated enough, to name our first daughter, Sarika.

Growing up in the 50's and 60's my greatest influences came from the Feminist Movement. Many of the leaders were Jewish women who were questioning Patriarchy and the systemic oppression of women. My parents were members of a progressive synagogue and the first rabbi that I remember marched with Dr. King and was arrested trying to integrate a lunch counter in St. Augustine, Florida. Women's rights and civil rights were bound together in my emerging Jewish identity. My mother was a fierce feminist caught in the structures of the *Feminine Mystique* of the 50's but she, and my father, wanted something better for their four daughters.

There were no women rabbis when I was growing up. The closest I got to experiencing female religious role models were seeing the huge statue of Mary at the Catholic school my friends attended and witnessing the awesome sight of the canonization of Elizabeth Seton in St. Peters Square at the Vatican. As an undergraduate, I met Betty Friedan just as the first woman was about to be ordained as a rabbi in 1972. She asked me if I was going to be a rabbi. I responded that I would never want to be a token in a Patriarchal profession! And God laughed! Or maybe it was Sarah laughing, again. A few years later I was accepted into rabbinical school. I went to seminary thinking that it would further my personal spiritual journey but still never imagined myself as a rabbi serving a community. I also remember thinking that I would meet other women who wanted to challenge systems of oppression based on gender and race and would share my commitment to social justice because this is what I believed the teachings of Judaism to be grounded in. I found that there were few role models who shared my passions, and my feminist theory antennae put up barriers to my own deepening in the toolbox of Jewish tradition and my own growth. This is where humility and the opportunity to be part of something greater than myself broke down my resistance and helped me to see that beneath the layers of Patriarchy was a tradition rich with relevance and meaning.

Seminary in the late 70's was challenging. As a member of one of the first classes of women, they had not even thought through accessibility to rest rooms. Most the professors were from Europe and had never imagined that they would be teaching women for the rabbinate. Many were skeptical at best and we had to prove ourselves. There were times it felt like a men's locker room because the culture did not fit us in language or style. I remember writing a paper on a rabbinic text about rape. The text said that if a woman is raped in a field she is to be believed and she is not presumed guilty of adultery but if she is raped in the city she is presumed guilty of adultery. The reasoning of generations of male commentators explained that if she screamed out in the field, she may not have been heard but if she screamed in the city, surely she would have been heard and rescued. Around the same time Susan Brownmiller's groundbreaking book on women and rape called *Against our Will* was published. I used her research to critique the rabbinical commentary and the texts saying that many women do not scream in the city or the field because screaming would put their lives at risk. I was told that I should keep my feminist comments to myself. I also helped to found the first infant care cooperative in the workplace in the state of Ohio at my seminary because the first female student who was pregnant could not find quality affordable child care for her child. Male students and their families were using substandard child care because their priority was their professional development. Not so for the women. The wellbeing of our children came first.

My feminist lens influences everything I do and am. As a mother and grandmother, I put the health and wellbeing of my children and my family first. This has shaped my workplace where I support this value for all of our staff and for the male rabbis as well. I have the wonderful opportunity and challenge of making sure that the voices and names of women throughout the tradition are heard and spoken. The genre of midrash has allowed us to hear the laugh of Sarah, expound on the cries of Hagar and Rebecca and explore the relationships of the sisters Rachel and Leah and of so many other biblical and post biblical women whose stories can be told more fully now that women are adding our experience and perspectives to the ongoing story of Torah. Rituals that were overlooked like the onset of menstruation, the loss of a miscarriage or an abortion or the beginning of menopause can now become part of the life cycle events that mark meaningful moments in our lives. Liberating the language of naming God as male also continues to free us to claim our place as central in religious experience.

I also find that people are less guarded and more open to express feelings with me. This has opened a world of deepened pastoral care for women and for men. I also hope that as a woman I have opened the possibilities for other women to imagine themselves serving in ways we have not been able to in the past.

In the beginning there were people who would not even consider a woman guiding and serving as a rabbi for their life cycle events. This has dramatically changed over the 40 years I have been serving as a rabbi. The #metoo movement is an important sign that women's experiences and voices matter. Many of us understand that sexual harassment is a way that the culture tries to stifle our voices and challenge our equal participation by taking our power. I am proud that there is a generation of women that is able to call this for what it is. When I began as a rabbi calling out this behavior could have ended my career. Today we will not let that happen. I believe that women serving as clergy in many religious denominations is helping to level the playing field for women everywhere.

One of the holiest and yes, also painful and controversial moments in our sanctuary at Central Reform Congregation, was the ordination of the Womenpriests. Two women who were practicing Roman Catholics and serving communities approached me. They wanted a sacred place to share their ordination and no church was open to them. I knew that there were core issues like abortion that separated us but when they explained that many people told them to be ordained as Episcopalians or even as another denomination of Catholics I could not turn them away. They explained that they were Roman Catholic, it is who they were and how they felt they needed to serve. I understood that. Many people I admired urged me to be ordained in another less Patriarchal religious tradition. That didn't work for me either. I was a Jewish woman and wanted to serve my faith community as they did.

The ordination of the Womenpriests was a humble and grace-filled ceremony presided over by a woman who had been a Dominican Sister in South Africa for forty five years. When she was ordained a bishop by other male bishops to be able to bring women into the priesthood, she lost everything. She lost her home, her pension, (she had been a homiletics professor for many generations of priests) and she lost her community of sisters. But there she was ordaining these two women and

opening up a world to people who had felt on the margins
for so long: the queer community, the disability community
and so many who longed to be included in the ceremony,
in the sacred. We stood at the opening of the tent that day
and she invited all of us to keep it open. It felt to me that she
invited all of us to become priests, not in any one theology
or faith tradition, but she invited all of us to become priests
and priestesses, every one of us ordained to take the ordinary
and raise it up with ceremony with devotion with practice and
with preparation. This is the promise of feminism: to open
all worlds, all possibilities to everyone and to see the infinite
worth and potential for holiness in everyone.

I have had many moments where I have had the opportunity to stand at the opening of the tent, often in the heat of
the day as a rabbi. I have had the privilege to dedicate my life
to the repairing of the world, by speaking up and showing up
and changing the paradigm using everything I have; privilege,
torah and the Jewish story I carry in my bones.

It has been 40 years since I began this journey and I
wouldn't change any of it. I met my husband the first day of
rabbinical school in Jerusalem and together we had 3 children
and two grandchildren who take our breadth away and know
that they come first.

I am part of a congregation that created a work place that
shares a feminist egalitarian vision that supports me as a working

mother, and that values complete inclusivity, radical hospitality and the possibility of the awakening of compassion in everything, absolutely everything, that we do. As a woman and as a rabbi I have had the opportunity to build relationships that work together to bend the arc toward justice for women, for the gay lesbian and transgendered community, and for our black and brown sisters and brothers who are Jews and non-Jews, alike. Together we bring the voices of my silent sisters in the texts to life.

I am grateful for all the holy opportunities I have had on the street as a rabbi who stands with those who will not rest until black lives matter. Who proclaim daily that until all are free, no one is free. Torah demands that we change the paradigm to change the world and we have much work still to do as we stand in the opening of the tent.

Looking back, however, the proudest moments for me are the quiet ones that no one really sees. Standing beside another bat mitzvah, officiating at gay and trans weddings, sitting at the bedside of someone who is dying who has no one else to accompany them and now, sharing the agony of other parents who have lost a child and helping them through the impossible. I am also proud of the community we have built that is willing to be a sanctuary for and put our bodies on the line for those who are marginalized like the refugees and immigrants seeking asylum on our borders. And I am grateful for my relationships with other religious women, too numerous to mention, women like Sister Carla Mae Streeter, who dare to stand at the opening of the tent and weave new garments that honor and include us all.

Carla Mae: That is quite a story, Susan, and it explains so well what has shaped your heart. It has been a formation indeed, insights, meanings, and values that have set you on a course-for-others, especially those on the fringes.

My own story continues to amaze me each time I recall it and try to share it. I was born of a devout Catholic family in Milwaukee, Wisconsin, back in 1937. Around age 12 I had an experience that remains with me to this day. I was sitting in a movie...the old "King of Kings" film, and I suddenly realized that this character named Jesus that I was learning about in religion class was real. I guess you'd call it going from 'knowing in the head' to 'knowing in the gut.' I remember being so stunned by this realization that I left the movie under cover of darkness and went over to the parish church. I sat down in the back to ponder this discovery. My faith had taught me that this Jesus, risen and living transformed humanness, was present under the form of consecrated bread in the little box or 'tabernacle' of the church. So I started up a conversation. "So, you're really real, are you? Not just a character in a story? OK, if that's so, then you are God-in-my-flesh, and that's amazing. I can't think of a better direction for my little life than to make you the center of it. So, that's what I am going to do." What came over me with this adolescent decision was a peace I cannot explain. It was as if I had psychologically hit a target of some kind.

What happened to mature this early choice was very healthy. I fell in love with a college student who was rooming and boarding with our family. I sensed what had happened to me, young as I was, and knew if it wasn't Eddie, it could very well be someone else that I could love and marry. But when I weighed the two, my earlier choice and this possibility, I always came up with the realization, that for me, marrying someone I could really love wouldn't be enough. I would always go back to seeking that One who had made that earlier claim on me.

Early on, in high school, I sought out a group of women who were on the same search as I was. I entered a community of Dominican women and began formation in Dominican spirituality to pursue my search, but here is where the story becomes a holy trick. I was a deeply introverted young girl. I often helped other students privately because I had a good mind, but when I would stand up to give a class report, I would fall to pieces. I could not speak in public. So what caught my attention was a picture in the information folder for these Dominican women, of a sister in a chicken coup taking care of chickens. Now I was a great animal lover, and thought to myself: "There...that's what I can do. I can take care of those chickens, and I won't have to talk to anybody." In my immaturity, I didn't realize that I had been led to the Dominican Order. In the Catholic community, this is the Order of PREACHERS. Well, the One I was seeking winked, and played a holy trick

A priest from a rural little parish visited the community to request sisters for his little country school. He met with the community and made his request. The community gave him four sisters to start the school. I listened, and what rose up in me was a tremendous indignation that these children had no one to teach them. Something snapped within me, and as I remember it, it was something I felt like the dissolving of a blockage. I went to English class the next day, and we were assigned an 'interview' process with a class partner. One of us was to be a famous person, the other the interviewer. This should have terrified me, because I would have to stand before the class in one of these two roles. Instead, my partner and I put on the craziest slap-stick routine the class had ever heard, as we interviewed Queen Elizabeth of England. The sister invited us out into the hallway, and said, "Well! I certainly didn't intend this assignment to be a slap-stick comedy routine!" I said nothing, but quietly thought to myself, "I don't care. This was my 'coming out' party." From that day on my tongue was loosed. I speak my truth, But I know it is possible because something in me was healed by the One I have set my heart on.

I later made my religious vows into the hands of the sister who taught us English, as she had become the president of our community. I continued my formation, completing a first degree in Music Education (I play the accordion), then going on to do a masters in Sacred Studies and doctoral work in Theology. I have ministered through teaching and preaching since 1960, helping others to teach, preach, minister, and lead. I especially get great joy out of watching timid students, eyes full of fear, gain confidence to write and speak. Perhaps because I recognize my former self in their fear.

My ministry has been directed to freeing others up to confidently search out the truth of scripture, of Catholic belief, and find out where it originated, why it is plausible, and how it can be expanded and communicated best. This has led me to dialogue with members of the scientific community, and to members of the ecumenical and interfaith community. Thus, my years of dialogue with Susan, and deep friendships with others who do not share my same experiences. It has been a holy trick indeed. Anyone who thinks the Great Mystery of the Universe has no sense of humor had better think again. I am evidence.

And so, Susan and I have completed these conversations with you. Hopefully you have found pieces of truth that have resonated with your deepest hopes and dreams. Be ready for holy tricks...be prepared to think possible what you might dismiss as unlikely or impossible. We see through a glass darkly...we see only partially. We see through a physics that we know. We cannot ever imagine an alternative physics, one different than the one our laws follow. Our greatest mistake is to fall into *the sin of certitude*...thinking we have all the truth about something. A subtle form of idolatry, we fall into the self-worship that keeps us confined in our own limited perspectives. Yes, we are tentatively certain of facts, scientific and sacred. But given new data, we need to be ready to be off once again, expanding the truth we had, making room for a fuller understanding, until we are before that Mystery that holds it all. Then all of us will know...even as we are known.

THE BROKEN
AND THE WHOLE

"And the people collected the broken tablets and carried
them alongside of the whole"
(Talmud, Shekalim 1:1)

Susan: Looking back over the chapters that span decades of discourse we find ourselves in a post 9/11, post Ferguson, post "#metoo" and post Trump world. We have marched together on the streets for a living wage and for Medicaid expansion. We have stood firm in our common command to welcome the stranger as we fight for the human rights of immigrants and refugees. We have traveled to the border and beyond to witness the horror of families separated and children in cages. We have used our voices to demand that the systems of oppression that criminalize poverty and race and gender and sexual orientation give way to a new paradigm that sees God in everyone. We have pleaded on behalf of Mother Earth as the climate crisis threatens our future. We have taken long enough to finish this book to live to see a Pope affirm the rights of the Queer community to celebrate civil unions. We have continued to struggle with our own beliefs as reproductive freedom is threatened.

Carla Mae: We have indeed, Susan. We make no claim to settling all these issues. Instead, we offer them just as they are, in process of always seeking out a fuller truth. We dishonor them if we freeze any partial advance and call it done. One of the most beautiful aspects of our dialogue together is the discovery that our humanness is always walking into a fuller truth, and so we need to be ready for surprises. There have been surprises all along the way. We have learned from one another that what we thought was true, wasn't or was true only under certain circumstances. This has humbled both of us. We have made a good start at avoiding the sin of certitude.

Susan: We have held each other through the personal sorrow of losing a daughter and dear friends through the years. We have suffered the collective shame of clergy who would dare to abuse children. We have rejoiced when new life and new chapters with new relationships and opportunities unfold before us. These events have frayed the new garment we have been weaving together over the years, but it remains strong because it dares to defy the delusion of separateness. Our new garment remains woven of the courageous conversations and deep love and respect we have for each other.

What began as an opportunity to model civility to redeem an ancient disputation has become a book filled with ideas that break through stereotypes and demonstrate how religious women bring new insights to old texts. We have found that our conversations bring the voices of our foremothers alive through our experiences as women and we have begun to weave a new garment.

Carla Mae: We have learned to forgive and go on, but we must not forget the rancor and abuse of the past, or we will repeat it, so fragile are we. The foolishness of the past must stand as a warning sentry, keeping us from the disrespect and abuse that was real in our past. Instead, women's voices can be prophetic, for we speak from the very abuse we warn against.

Susan: Our new garment defies the sin of certitude and dares to include the broken with the whole. We have learned how to hold together different ways of reaching toward the holy with strands of deep listening, feminist principles, and our commitment to the common good over self-interest.

Our new garment is radically inclusive. No one is left out of its weaving and all are equally valued. There is no room to make any strand less important than any other, regardless of its color or strength or source.

Our new garment is made up of a whole that able is to celebrate and appreciate the beauty of the strands that we are drawn to without feeling that we need to change or discard the others.

Our new garment is able to hold the embodiment of godliness within the experience of human sexuality expressed in different ways as long as there is no tolerance for the abuse of power. We hold the strands together with the humility needed to pave the way for change from the inclusion of women in all aspects of ministry to the recognition of the rights of the LGBTQ community to all the sacred spaces we have to offer.

Our new garment makes room for the belief that we share that the soul does exist beyond this world but that this belief is beyond certainty and requires faith. We dare to weave together this garment with wisdom vowing to make room for courageous conversations around reproductive freedom guided by compassion.

Our new garment includes the words, **Black Lives Matter**, to begin to unravel the centuries of white supremacy that continue to hold us back from the systemic changes needed in all areas of our lives. Weaving our garment has created a safe space for discussions on how our sacred texts demonize the other and feed anti-Semitism, islamophobia, homophobia and racism in all its forms. We hope that our new garment will call into question the rituals and stories that tip the scales toward judgment over mercy.

Carla Mae: As we complete this work, woven of years and losses, struggles and successes, we find before us in this time of the pandemic, a significant writing that cheers us on. Francis, leader of the Catholic community has just issued *Fratelli Tutti*, an encyclical addressed to all the earth's peoples of good will. As I read it I found myself thinking that he had sneaked a preview of our book and was nodding. His first chapter is a scathing exposure to what you and I have been railing against for years. One of his solutions? Sincere and open dialogue. He speaks of a new kind of loving. We are in good company, Susan. We have made a beginning.

Susan: We recognize that this garment is woven of our own life stories and struggles over thirty years. We hope that our conversations inspire others to weave new garments with unlikely partners that will take us to a more inclusive and loving place with each other.

For now, we pray that our new garment can be a worthy covering for the Soul of the soul, the God that fills us with hope that the good in us will win.